Y0-BDC-629

# Walking
# the
# Edge

# Walking the Edge

A Day Hiker's Guide to Northeast
Arizona's White Mountain Trails
in and near Show Low.

Laurie Dee Acree

© 2004 by Laurie Dee Acree. All rights reserved. No part of this book may be reproduced in any form, or by electronic, mechanical, or other means, without permission in writing from the publisher and author.

Although the author has exhaustively researched all sources to ensure the accuracy and completeness of the information contained in this book, she assumes no responsibility for errors, inaccuracies, omissions, or any inconsistency herein. Any slights of people, places or organizations are unintentional.

All maps, artwork, design, composition and photographs are by the author. Published in Canada.

Ten percent of proceeds earned from the sale of this book will be donated to the T.R.A.C.K.S organization who create and maintain trails within the White Mountain Trail System.

To order more copies of this book, please write or call the author during business hours. An Order Form is also included on the last page of this book to mail in requests. Thank you.

**National Library of Canada Cataloguing in Publication**

Acree, Laurie Dee
Walking the edge / Laurie Dee Acree.
ISBN 1-4120-1111-6
I. Title.
GV199.42.A72S56 2004    796.51'09791'35        C2003-904539-0

**TRAFFORD**

**This book was published** *on-demand* **in cooperation with Trafford Publishing.** On-demand publishing is a unique process and service of making a book available for retail sale to the public taking advantage of on-demand manufacturing and Internet marketing. **On-demand publishing** includes promotions, retail sales, manufacturing, order fulfilment, accounting and collecting royalties on behalf of the author.

Suite 6E, 2333 Government St., Victoria, B.C. V8T 4P4, CANADA
Phone        250-383-6864        Toll-free     1-888-232-4444 (Canada & US)
Fax          250-383-6804        E-mail        sales@trafford.com
Web site     www.trafford.com    TRAFFORD PUBLISHING IS A DIVISION OF TRAFFORD HOLDINGS LTD.
Trafford Catalogue #03-1480     www.trafford.com/robots/03-1480.html

10          9          8          7          6          5          4          3

# DEDICATION

*"In everything give thanks to God" (1 Thess. 5:18).*

P<small>EANUTS</small>

I dedicate this book first of all to my Lord and Savior, Jesus Christ, who not only created all the beauty around me, but also my ability to appreciate it.

Next I would like to thank my husband for his support and for showing me how much fun it is to hike. Over the years we've hiked throughout the United States and Europe. I'd be amiss if I didn't mention my four-legged hiking buddies, Popcorn, Candy, and Pepsi; my dogs. And . . . a very special mention of my best friend, Peanuts. Peanuts was my Great Dane/German Shepherd mix who died on May 10, 1999, while this trail book was in its beginning stages. He walked a few of the trails mentioned, and I am grateful to God for the years we had together.

God answers prayers. In writing this book I have had need of computer hardware and the good Lord has seen to it that my prayers were quickly answered. My gratitude to Don and Sharon Keas who offered the free unlimited use and easy access of their computer hardware and to Glen Fisher who graciously found and installed an internal zip drive in my old PC enabling me to permanently save my work.

Lastly, my gratitude to the authors, Lonnie Burstein Hewitt and Barbara Coffin Moore, whose publication Walking San Diego inspired me to write my own book on hiking. The title for this book came from the Rim View trail which over looks the edge of the Mogollon Rim and of which the General Crook Trail intersects.

i

# ACKNOWLEDGMENTS

*"In the beginning God created the heaven and the earth"*
*(Genesis 1:1).*

It is my belief that I was inspired by and have had the help of God in creating this book, and I want to publicly thank the Lord for guiding me every step of the way on this project. It has been a significant part in my life since 1998 and many people have helped to make it possible. The best way to write a trail guide would be for me, as the author, to hike every trail, every year. I confess to falling short of that standard.

Many thanks to my husband who not only journeyed many of these trails with me, but encouraged me. My other cheerleaders were my parents and friends. They all had to put up with my monomania. My gratitude to the offices of the Chamber of Commerce, Parks & Recreation, TRACKS, and Forest Ranger Stations who were of help in my research. I would like to name a few of those individuals who significantly helped: Beth Puschel, Ruth Nelson, John Vuolo, and David Matthews. At the top of the list are the proofreaders, who worked through the entire manuscript or reviewed selected chapters: Ute Lamb, Nancee Hunter, and my husband, Al Reyes. The following are individuals who shared experiencing these trails with me: Al Reyes, Gail Lynn, Pat Mead, Martha Jorden, Ute Lamb, Dick & Sandra Williams, Val Muzzuco, Gracie Kelley, and Alice Owen.

Thanks to everyone!
Laurie Dee Acree

# CONTENTS

# PRE-HIKE

Fulfilling A Need
Using This Guide
A Word to the Hiker
High Altitude Caution
What to Do if Lost or Injured

## GENERAL CLIMATE

| | | |
|---|---|---|
| WINTER (Dec. - Feb.) | 46 $^F$ high<br>10 $^F$ low<br>5" precipitation | |
| SPRING (Mar. - May) | 63 $^F$ high<br>32 $^F$ low<br>4" precipitation | |
| SUMMER (June - Aug.) | 85 $^F$ high<br>52 $^F$ low<br>6" precipitation | |
| FALL (Sep. - Nov.) | 68 $^F$ high<br>26 $^F$ low<br>7" precipitation | |

Windy season is typically March through May.
Monsoon season is typically July and August.

# FULFILLING A NEED

*"My soul followeth hard after Thee: Thy right hand upholdeth me"*
*(Psalm 63:8).*

Hiking gives you something you can't get in an office, gym, or at home. Hiking gives you an environment you may not have known or may have forgotten. The outdoors, the sun, the air, the seasons of the year, walking is more than an exercise, it is a ticket to appreciating the world around you.

Each year, many thousands of visitors come to the White Mountains of Arizona. Over 16,250 people use the trails within the Lakeside Forest Service district per year, and this number doesn't take into account the trails being used within other local jurisdictions or managing agencies. Residents, as well as visitors, need an user-friendly and detailed book about the numerous trails that fall within a defined area. This guide fulfills that need and beyond addressing hikers' needs and information on the area and its wildlife communities.

Here are hikes, enough for days of fun outings. I've included some local history, information, and as many odd and interesting facts as I could fit in. You'll notice a blank box on every trail page. This was for you to write in your details about the hike.

# USING THIS GUIDE

*"For God so loved the world, that He gave His only begotten Son, that whoever believes in Him should not perish, but have eternal life" (John 3:16).*

The primary intent of this guide book is to provide information that will help hikers choose hiking ventures according to their desires and abilities, as well as a detailed description of each trail. It is intended to be used *in* conjunction with topographic maps, which can be purchased at ranger stations, gift and sporting goods stores or through the U. S. Geological Survey. The White Mountain Trail System (W.M.T.S.) has a basic trail booklet available through the city or ranger station. Additionally, the local White Mountain Independent newspaper periodically will feature a single trail in their Friday issue titled <u>Take A Hike</u> and they annually produce a Trail Guide encompassing a few local trails as well as others found randomly throughout a far greater range in the White Mountains. Both are good sources to use.

Hiking distances in this guide are not always exact. **One note of caution** - this guide will not be enough for you to navigate a trail if the governing agency or group doesn't regularly maintain the trail markers and trail signs on a trail. The main purpose of trail maps in this book are to get you to the trailhead and roughly give you the big picture of its route.

In this book, <u>Walking the Edge</u>, each trail is described with the following information:    Location, length, rate, time, directions, elevation, and direction to hike. Other given information will include parking, use, hiker's box, and comments. Next, a simplistic map of the feature hike is given. Show Low is considered the central point for directions.

The rating can be interpreted as follows: *Easy* trails can be completed without difficulty by hikers of all abilities; hikes rated *moderate* will challenge novices; and *hard* hikes will tax even experienced hikers. Trail distances given are that of my use of a pedometer, posted mileage, or from a publication by the managing agency.

The following are words or terms used in this book, which may need a bit of explaining to help anyone new to this area or just new to hiking in general.

**ACCESS TRAIL** - A trail created to take one from its beginning to a connector or main trail.

**A.K.A**. - Abbreviation to mean "also known as".

**ARRANGEMENT** - The trails are in alphabetical order within the alphabetized city order.

**BLUE DIAMONDS** - The bulk of the trails in this book are part of the White Mountain Trail System (W.M.T.S.). These trails are identified by the plastic blue diamonds nailed to trees along the trail's route. Diamonds with green dots indicate it as a 'connector' trail; yellow dots 'short cut'; red 'vista view'. Any two same color dots on a blue diamond indicate where the trail merges into another type.

**CONNECTOR TRAIL** - A trail that, if followed, will join a main trail. They do not have a kiosk (trailhead). Look for two green dots on a blue diamond if the trails is part of W.M.T.S..

**FR** - fire or forest road

**LINDEN** - An area of the county that lies between the cities of Show Low and Pinedale.

**MAPS** - The maps aren't to scale, but their proportions are generally correct. The main purpose of the maps are to get you to the trailhead. North is always up. The trail map generally follows its description.

**MCNARY** -This town is south a few miles of Pinetop and located on the White Mountain Indian Reservation.

**MILEAGE** - Driving distance and trail mileage was taken from published sources or from the author. For the most part, driving directions are given starting at the Show Low Post Office.

**PINETOP-LAKESIDE** - These two towns were incorporated together, but for purposes of this book I address them as individual towns. Lakeside begins where Wagon Wheel ends on its south side. Lakeside ends at its south side just on the other side of the of the White Mountain Village Shopping Center. Pinetop begins where Lakeside ends and stretches south to the Indian reservation.

**RATINGS** - I show hikes rated as easy, moderate, and hard. These ratings are based on my own reaction. I am a middle-age deskbound type, not a highly conditioned athlete who never tires. You won't hurt my feelings if you adjust my rating for your own fitness level.

**RISKS** - I avoid taking risks on hikes and none of these hikes require any risky climbing.

**SHORT LOOP** - Also called 'short cut.' An optional direction to take if you want a shorter hike.

**SHOW LOW POST OFFICE** - is located at 191 W. Deuce of Clubs Blvd at the corner of W. McNeil.

**SPUR TRAIL** - Is a short trail off a main one that takes you to a scenic view, usually at the top of a mountain. A sign is usually posted at the junction. May also be referred to as an 'access' trail.

**TERRAIN** - The country is generally benign. You shouldn't get lost in the woods if you stay on the trail.

**T.R.A.C.K.S.** - Acronym for **T**railsystem **R**ide **a**nd Cycle and **C**ross-Country Ski and **H**ike the **S**easons. Tracks started in 1992 branching off from the White Mountain Horsemen's Association. They are an umbrella organization of the Pinetop-Lakeside Parks and Recreation Department. The group consists of hikers, bikers, equestrians, and skiers.

**TRAILHEADS** - Those with limited parking are cindered pads with little to no turning radius. Larger ones will accommodate several cars and trailers. Trailheads usually have a sign with posted information and are also called kiosks.

**TRAILS** - Each trail described also includes a section where you can write in your own comments. In each section I've listed loop trails first followed by one way trails, connectors and then access trails.

**WAGON WHEEL** - the area of county that exists between the cities of Show Low and Lakeside. At the time of this writing, the cities of Pinetop/Lakeside and Show Low are considering splitting and absorbing this area into their respective city limits.

**WATER** - Don't count on finding water anywhere. Take it with you.

**W.M.T.S.** - Abbreviation for the 'White Mountain Trail System'.

# A WORD TO THE HIKER

*"Having therefore, brethren, boldness to enter into the holiest by the blood of Jesus" (Hebrews 10:19).*

Hiking is great exercise. The dictionary defines hiking as "to go on an extended walk for pleasure or exercise." Some of the trails in this guidebook are strolls while others feel more like hikes. Do take time out to listen to birds, smell a flower, make notes, or take photos.

The key to a successful hike is to plan ahead and be prepared. Hikers who underestimate the distance or time required to complete a trip may find themselves hiking in the dark. What you think will be a three hour hike can turn into a six-hour epic due to bad weather, injury or losing your way.

An experienced hiker traveling at a fast clip can generally make 2.5 miles per hour; perhaps more if the distance is all downhill. Novices and hikers in poor physical condition generally have a maximum speed of 1.5 miles per hour. And note that these rates don't include stops for rest and refreshment, which add tremendously to a hiker's enjoyment and appreciation of the surroundings.

Do take rest breaks at least every hour for 10+ minutes. For short hikes you can wear comfortable cushioned tennis or walking shoes with good tread. For longer hikes, over four miles, hiking boots are recommended. I recommend traveling below top speed, focusing more attention on the surrounding natural beauty and less on the exercise of hiking itself. Attitude, awareness, freedom, and satisfaction matter more than how far, how fast, or how high you climb. Hiking can bring you closer to the wilderness, closer to God, and closer to yourself.

To the best of my ability I have done what I could to verify the accuracy of the mileage of every trail. The Forest Service District rounds up their mileage. So you'll find, if you use a pedometer, that discrepancies may exist from as little as one tenth to one mile off. To help, for the most part, I have given the *time* it took me to hike the trail. A good tip is to always plan on setting the pace and distance of your daily hikes to the *slowest* member in your group. This rule is especially important when hiking with children or elderly people.

Safety is an important concern in all outdoor activities. No guidebook can alert you to every potential hazard there is or anticipate the limitation of every hiker. You assume responsibility for your own safety. Some of the problems you may face outdoors include: Minor cuts & scratches, insect bites, poisonous plants & snakes, pain from headaches & sore muscles, foot blisters, and sprains & bruises.

A cellular phone in your gear may prove invaluable. Always leave information with someone about where you will be going and how long you expect to be gone. Be sure you follow these plans. It is wise to keep informed on current weather conditions and exercise common sense.

Each hiker should bring all the water she or he will need; roughly a quart per person. A microscopic paramecium, *Giardia*, has forever changed the old custom of dipping for a fresh swallow from a cool brisk stream. The symptoms of "beaver fever" can commence up to a week or two after ingesting *Giardia* and are debilitating nausea and diarrhea.

Hiking activities depend on the forest conditions and possible fire restrictions, so please call the Lakeside Ranger District, 928) 368-5111, the Show Low Parks & Recreation Dept., 928) 537-2800, or Pinetop Parks and Recreation Dept., 928) 368-6700.

It is important to beware of the fact that the T.R.A.C.K.S organization meets year round and continuously maintain, change, create, and alter any blue diamond trails in the White Mountain Trail System.

## In Summary
* Be sure the forest is open.
* Be sure that you take appropriate maps and this book.
* If possible, include a cellular phone in your backpack.
* Use the buddy system. Take a friend.
* Always leave information with someone as to where you are going and how long you expect to be gone.
* Be sure to check that you have water and weather protection.
* Check the daily weather forecast before you leave. Be sure to allow yourself plenty of time.
* If provided, sign in at the kiosk's register.

# HIGH ALTITUDE CAUTION

*"O Give thanks unto the Lord, for He is good: for His mercy endures forever"*
*(Psalm 107:1).*

If you are not used to being at mid-high altitude then be forewarned. Hikes in this book start at about 6200' and go up from there. At higher elevations, the air pressure is low, causing your body to get 1/4 to 1/3 less oxygen than at sea level.

High altitudes mean:
1. You won't have the energy you are used to.
2. Hiking will be a lot harder on your heart.
3. You will be thirstier than usual.
4. You will sunburn more easily.
5. It will be much colder than normal, especially at night.

Altitude affects hikers differently. Watch for signs of altitude sickness such as headaches, impaired memory, and extreme shortness of breath. The body can partially compensate for the "thinner" air, but acclimation takes weeks. Early signs of altitude sickness are a headache and slight nose-bleed. Especially with children, be on the lookout for it. Rest often; descend if condition persists. Those use to lower elevations should take special care not to overexert. Start out slowly and work up that big hike.

# WHAT TO DO IF LOST OR INJURED

*"Forgive us our sins, for we also forgive everyone who sins against us and lead us not into temptation" (Luke 11:4).*

Be sure to check frequently for landmarks by which to return should you somehow get turned around in the forest. Don't wander about. Sit down, relax and very carefully try to run through your mind the events that led up to your becoming lost. If you have plenty of daylight left, travel slowly in the direction you feel is correct. Make sure that if you had been climbing that you now travel only downhill. If you come to a stream, do not leave it unless, of course, you have found your trail. A stream almost always leads to civilization.

Keep a very close eye on the remaining daylight. If the day is going to end soon, you should immediately find a place to camp overnight.

Gather whatever rocks or stones are available, place them in a circle to make a place for a safe fire and gather a supply of wood. You should have a fire burning by the time it becomes dark, eaten whatever food you have allowed for your meal and know where everything in your camp is located.

If you can't build a fire and do not have a blanket or bedroll then cover yourself with sticks and leaves to escape the cold and wind; it works!

If you are injured and cannot travel, then a signal fire is your best bet. A very smoky fire by day and a bright fire at night has the best chance of bringing results. Can you see how important the contents of your day or back pack can become? **A note of warning:** In case of extreme fire conditions in the forest making any kind of a fire could be considered illegal.

Pet buddy, Peanuts, on the Ice Cave Trail

# ORIENTATION

Our State & National Trail History
The Majestic White Mountains of Arizona
Local Trails

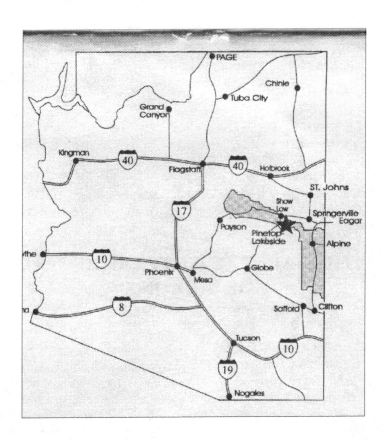

**State Map of Arizona**

# OUR STATE & NATIONAL
# TRAIL HISTORY
*"Man shall not live by bread alone..." (Matthew 4:4).*

Trails have quite a legacy in Arizona originating with trails built and used by Native Americans. Additional routes were established by Spanish explorers and missionaries from the early 1500s through the early 1700s. Fur traders began establishing trails as early as 1825. Beginning in 1846, many military and migration trails were established across present-day Arizona.

In the early 1900s Forest Reserves (known today as National Forests) were established and networks of trails were developed primarily for horse travel. These early trails were established for range management and wildfire prevention, and others for recreational purposes.

The Arizona State Trails System (ASTS) was established in the late 1970s as an attempt to inventory trails in Arizona that met set criteria. As of the late 1990s there are almost 600 trails in the ASTS, totaling approximately 6,000 miles.

The National Forest has over 950 miles of trails. Many trails are maintained through the hard work of volunteers. They offer beautiful vistas, varying physical challenges, and chances to enjoy our Nation's past.

# THE MAJESTIC WHITE MOUNTAINS
# OF ARIZONA
*"Blessed are the poor in spirit: for theirs is the kingdom of heaven"*
*(Matthew. 5:3).*

In the late 1800s settlers were lured to this area by its abundance of natural resources - open pastures, sparkling lakes and streams and its tall evergreen pine trees. Museums, archaeological ruins, and historical points of interest offer a glimpse into the culture and history of the region's founders.

The lush pine and aspen forests envelop miles of maintained trails for hunting, hiking, horseback riding, mountain biking, and breathtaking scenic views. Other outdoor activities include golfing, water sports, bird watching, fishing, and picnicking.

# LOCAL TRAILS

*"Honor and majesty are before Him: strength and beauty are in His sanctuary"*
*(Psalm 96:6).*

Designated trails that fall on the forest service land in this area are named, assigned numbers, and customarily become part of the White Mountain Trail System. Look for the plastic blue diamonds nailed to trees. Trails on city land may also be part of the W.M.T.S. and have blue diamonds, however they aren't assigned a number. Any other managing agency outside this system will rely on their own type of signs.

Be aware that signs bearing the name and/or number of the trail should be present at trail junctions, although weathering and inconsiderate visitors sometimes ruin these plaques.

Spreading in and out from Show Low, the areas covered in this book range from Clay Springs/Pinedale in the west, to Vernon in the east, and Pinetop-Lakeside in the south. There is one exception, that being, the trails south of Pinetop that exist between McNary and Vernon (Los Burros, Lake Mountain) along FR 224. I have listed them under Vernon.

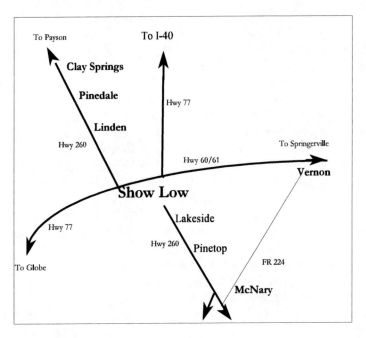

## The White Mountain Trail System

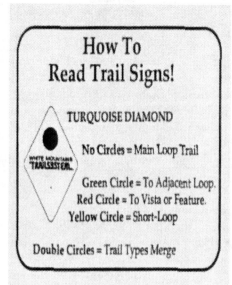

How To
Read Trail Signs!

TURQUOISE DIAMOND

No Circles = Main Loop Trail

WHITE MOUNTAINS
TRAILSYSTEM.

Green Circle = To Adjacent Loop.
Red Circle = To Vista or Feature.
Yellow Circle = Short-Loop

Double Circles = Trail Types Merge

In February of 1987, a group of 25 horsemen met to discuss the increasing loss of their riding areas. From this meeting formed the foundation of what is today over 200 miles of interconnected, multi-use trails known as the White Mountains Trail System (W.M.T.S.). The W.M.T.S. offers a variety of trail opportunities both in scenic beauty and skill levels.

Eventually the majority of the loop trails will be interconnected. When completed, ideally, one could journey from the Ghost of the Coyote trail (Pinedale) to Juniper Ridge to Los Caballos (Linden) to Buena Vista (Show Low) to Timber Mesa (Lakeside) to the Ice Cave to Blue Ridge (Pinetop) to Springs to Country Club to Los Burros (McNary/Vernon) to Land of the Pioneers (Vernon). Not all of this work has been done at the writing of this book (1998-2003). However, a good part of it has been. In Pinedale, one can hike from Juniper Ridge to Los Caballos to Buena Vista in Show Low. Then, in Lakeside, one can transverse from the Ice Cave to Blue Ridge to Springs to Country Club to Los Burros to Land of the Pioneers in Vernon. What is still to be done is the connectors between Ghost of the Coyote and Juniper Ridge; Buena Vista and Timber Mesa; Timber Mesa to Ice Cave.

Trails are designed to preserve the land, vegetation, and wildlife. All are accessible to hikers, and with a few exceptions, to bikers, cross-country skiers, and horseback riders. All of these trails are for non-motorized travel. Please report violations to the appropriate agency. A report form is provided at the back of this book.

Trails within the W.M.T.S. are marked with plastic blue diamonds nailed to trees. Yellow dots attached to the blue diamond indicate a short route back to the trailhead. Green ones indicate a connector trail to another W.M.T.S. loop and red ones indicate a special feature.

The blue diamonds should be spaced along the trail as to provide confirmation of the trail you are on. Directional arrows may also be used. Ideally, diamonds with trail loop number are located at trailheads and underneath the first diamond leaving the trailhead and, thereafter, spaced evenly half to three quarters of a mile along the trial. They should also be placed at road and trail junctions. Realistically, you will find the actual trails lacking a bit in this idealized system. Vandalism is its number one enemy. Volunteers are needed to maintain trails. Won't you consider helping out the TRACKS organization? Their goal is to *"use, promote, preserve, and protect the multi-use trails throughout Pinetop-Lakeside and the White Mountains."* They strive to support and assist the development, maintenance, and improvement of non-motorized trails. To get involved, you can call the Pinetop Lakeside Chamber of Commerce at 928) 368-6700.

Partnerships with the U. S. Forest Service, Pinetop/Lakeside TRACKS volunteer organization and The AZ State Parks Heritage Trails Fund have helped build these trails. The W.M.T.S. is more than trails, its really people who want to preserve the very reason they chose these mountains to call home: a love of nature. Let's help by doing our share of not destroying or littering them. Every little bit counts!

## Other Trail Markers

Rock Cairns ~ are a type of trail marker constructed along a trail where the posting of signs is not possible or desirable. Although I haven't noticed many of them, a rock cairn's dimensions should be approximately 18 inches in diameter at the base, piled 12 inches high, tapering to 9 inches at the top. Placement is usually within line-of-sight, that is, the next one is usually visible in the distance.

Chevrons ~ are V-shaped metal tags nailed to trees. Many miles of the General Crook Trail are marked with rock cairns and white and yellow V-shaped chevrons that were placed on trees in the late 1970's in a special project by the Boy Scouts of America.

## How to Follow a Faint Path

In the case of an extremely overgrown trail, markings of any kind may be impossible to find. On such a trail, the techniques used to build a trail serve as clues to its location. Well-constructed trails have rather wide, flat beds. Let your feet seek the flat spots when traveling through tall brush, and you will almost always find yourself on the trail. Look for other rock work that may have been placed to prevent erosion. Old sawed logs from previous trail maintenance can be used to navigate in spots where the trail bed is obscured; if you find a sawed log, then you must be on a trail that was maintained at some point in time. Switchbacks are also a sure sign of an official trail; wild game travels in straight lines, and horsemen traveling off-trail seldom bother to zigzag across hillsides. Previous travelers can also leave clues to the location of old trails; watch for footprints or hoof marks as you travel.

# REFERENCES

Trails Listed by Miles
Trails Listed by City
What to Take

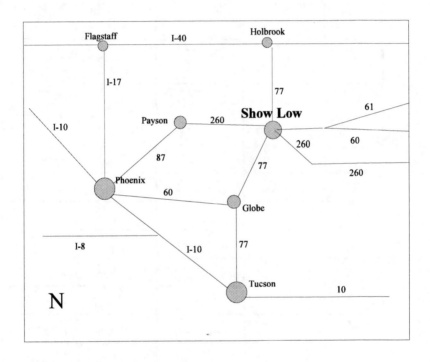

**Northeast portion of Arizona**

**Rough Distances in Hours to Show Low**
2 ½ hrs from Flagstaff
3 ½ hrs from Phoenix
4 hrs from Tucson
2 hrs from Payson

# TRAILS LISTED BY MILES*

(and W.M.T.S. designated trail numbers)

| Loop Trails | | | |
|:---:|:---:|:---:|:---:|
| MILES | RATE | LOCATION | TRAIL NAME |
| 1 | Easy+ | Lakeside | Rim View #615 |
| 1.1 | Easy+ | Show Low | Show Low City Park Walk |
| 1.2 | Easy + | Pinetop | Lake Walk *Woodland Lake Park* |
| 1.5 | Easy | Pinetop | Laurie's Delight *Bill Creek Trails Park* |
| 2 | Easy | Pinetop | Hitching Post *Woodland Lake Park* |
| 3.5 | Moderate | Pinetop | Country Club #632 |
| 3.8 | Easy | Pinetop | Springs #633 |
| 6 | Easy | Lakeside | Timber Mesa #636 |
| 8.6 | Moderate | Lakeside | Panorama #635 |
| 8.7 | Moderate | Pinetop | Blue Ridge #107 |
| 9 | Moderate | Show Low | Buena Vista #637 |
| 11 | Moderate | Vernon (McNary) | Land of the Pioneers #629 |
| 13 | Moderate | Vernon (McNary) | Los Burros #631 |
| 14 | Hard | Pinedale | Juniper Ridge #640 |
| 14+ | Hard | Linden | Los Caballos #638 |

| | | | |
|---|---|---|---|
| 16 | Hard | Pinedale | Ghost of the Coyote #641 |

## One Way Trails

| | | | |
|---|---|---|---|
| .29 | Easy | Pinetop | Meadow View *Woodland Lake Park* |
| .4 | Easy | Show Low | Show Low Lake |
| .5 | Moderate | Pinetop | Walnut Creek *Woodland Lake Park* |
| .5 | Easy | Pinetop | Old Hatchery |
| 1 | Easy | Pinetop | Turkey Track *Woodland Lake Park* |
| 1.9 | Easy+ | Show Low | Summit Sidewalk |
| 2.0 | Easy | Show Low | Fool Hollow Lake |
| 3.5 | Easy | Lakeside | Ice Cave #608 |
| 114 | Hard | Clay Springs | General Crook #130 |

*Connector, access, spur trails, nature study areas, or lookout towers are not included in the above list.*

**+** *Denotes a paved, wheel chair accessible trail.*

# TRAILS LISTED BY CITY
## Loops, Connectors, Accesses, & Spurs

<u>Clay Springs</u>
*General Crook - 1 way*

<u>Lakeside</u>
*Ice Cave - 1 way*
*Panorama Loop*
*Rim View Loop*
*Timber Mesa Loop*
*The Flume Connector*
*The Sawmill Connector*

<u>Linden</u>
*Ghost of the Coyote Loop*
*Los Caballos Loop*
*The Chihuahua Pine Connector*

<u>Pinedale</u>
*Juniper Ridge Loop*
*Juniper Ridge / General Crook Connector*
*The Lookout Connector*

<u>Pinetop</u>
*Blue Ridge Loop*
*Country Club Loop*
*Iron Horse Connector*
*Hitching Post Loop*
*Hitching Post / Big Springs Connector*
*Lake Walk Loop*
*Laurie's Delight Loop*
*Meadowview - 1 way*
*Old Hatchery Bridge - 1 way*
*Pinecrest "Access"*
*Springs Loop*
*Turkey Track - 1 way*
*Vista View Spur*
*Walnut Creek - 1 way*

Show Low
  *Buena Vista Loop*
  *Fool Hollow Lake - 1 way*
  *Show Low Lake - 1 way*
  *Show Low City Park Loop*
  *Summit Sidewalk - 1 way*

Vernon
  *Eckes Mountain Spur*
  *Land of the Pioneers Loop*
  *Los Burros Loop*
  *Chipmunk Springs Connector*
  *Four Springs at Lake*
    *Mountain Access*
  *Four Springs Connector*

*For a listing of trails by their trail number see Appendix B.*

## Easy Mileage Reference from Show Low

*DISTANCES are in MILES and are ROUNDED UP*

From Show Low, <u>junctions </u>of Hwys 77, 60, 61, & 260 (corner of gas station & Victorian bldg.) west on Hwy 260 to:
  *Linden, 5    Pinedale, 13    Clay Springs, 15*

From Show Low's <u>Post Office </u>east on the Deuce of Clubs to the inter-section of White Mtn. Road *(Bank of America & Bank One)* is one mile.

From <u>Intersection </u>of Deuce of Clubs & White Mountain Road south on Hwy 260 to:
  *Lakeside, 8    Pinetop, 12    Hon Dah, 15    McNary, 18*

From Show Low's <u>Post Office </u>staying on the Deuce of Clubs (Hwy 60) east to: *Vernon, 19.5* (There are no highway markers designating the distance to Vernon. After traveling the 19.5 miles keep your eye out for the gas station on your right.)

# WHAT TO TAKE

*"They were also to stand every morning to thank and praise the Lord. They were to do the same in the evening. . . " (1 Chronicles 23:30).*

Most hikers realize the importance of a good checklist once they are on the trail. What you have forgotten to pack may turn out to be only an inconvenience, or may pose a serious problem. A good checklist will help you remember the essentials.

The list below is only a suggested list. Use it to create your own, based on the nature of your hike and personal needs. Items will vary depending on how long you will be backpacking. Select items judiciously, with weight in mind.

## DAY HIKER'S CHECKLIST

_____ Identification
_____ This book and other trail or topo maps
_____ A friend
_____ Water (min. of two quarts per day/per person)
_____ A small backpack
_____ Small bottle of insect repellant
_____ Sunscreen, sunglasses
_____ Windbreaker, rain poncho
_____ A few band-aids & small tube of antiseptic
_____ Plastic baggies & toilet paper
_____ Food
_____ Small plastic bag to pack out trash
_____ Head covering (scarf, cap, hat)

## OTHER CONSIDERATIONS:

Cellular phone
Binoculars
Camera
Long pair of pants
Insulating stocking cap
Small flashlight
Notepad & pencil
Pedometer
Nutritional bars
Sports drink

Whistle
Compass
Walking stick
Medicines or prescriptions
Lighter or matches
Moleskin
Lip salve
Extra food & water
Extra warm clothing & socks
Signal mirror

# BACKPACKER'S LIST

*In addition to* packing the items mentioned for a day hike, for backpacking purposes you should consider the following:

**CLOTHING** — long sleeve shirt, insulated vest, warm jacket with hood

**FOOTWEAR** — hiking boots, lightweight camp shoes

**BEDDING** — sleeping bag, space blanket, foam pad or air mattress, pillow (deflating), ground cloth (plastic or nylon), tent, extra tent stakes

**COOKING** — 1 quart plastic water container, 1 gallon collapsible water container, backpack stove with extra fuel, funnel or pour sprout for fuel, fuel, aluminum foil, cooking pot, skillet, plateware, utensils, butane lighter or waterproof matches with container, can opener, wooden spoons, thermos bottle, potholder,

**FOOD & DRINK** — cereal, bread and/or crackers, trail mix, margarine, powered soups, spices, main course meals, powdered milk, drink mixes

**PHOTOGRAPHY** — extra film, accessories, dry bag

**MISCELLANEOUS** — shovel, toothpaste & brush, comb, water filter or purifier, first aid kit, pocket knife, insect repellant, spare batteries, candles, biodegradable soap, towel & wash cloth, waterproof covering for pack, sewing kit, extra shoe laces, handi-wipes, candles, playing cards, sunglasses, emergency phone numbers, medical card, extra cash, rope, duct tape, seam sealer, lightweight reading material, notepad & pen, laundry detergent, small scissors, safety pins, rubber bands, eye drops, talcum powder, small bell

If not included in your first aid kit, you might want to consider taking along:

Aspirin *(thins blood for high altitude sickness)*
Ibuprofen *(anti-inflammatory for muscles)*
Antacid tablets *(for high altitude sickness)*
Elastic wrap bandage & small instant ice pack *(for twisted or sprained ankles)*
Stingease *(for insect bites)*

To organize, separate all of your items into two piles. One pile for daily convenience (sunglasses, camera, map, snacks, etc.) and one pile for your destination camp. Store non-essential stuff down and deep; keep convenience items handy. Color code your stuff sacks (red for clothing; blue for food, etc). Internal frame backpacks carry weight low. Store hardware to the outside and use the side pockets for convenience items. Empty 35mm canisters are good for medicines and spices.

## Backpacking Tips:
* Plan to wash clothes on the trail rather than pack extra changes.
* Eliminate boxes, cans, jars etc. by carrying only the amounts you need in ziploc plastic baggies (i.e., one meal per bag).
* Pack extra candles, instead of heavy flashlight and batteries.
* Take one heavy duty plastic bag per person to act as emergency raingear or tarp.
* An old shower curtain makes a good ground cloth for your tent.

**Good Bear Scares** ~ Bears don't want a confrontation with humans anymore than hikers want to meet them on the trail. The key is to let the bear know you're around before you meet. A good bear scare is to attach a small bell to your pack.

**Foot Care Advice** ~ Treat blisters caused from shoes or boots by cleaning feet, applying antiseptic and gauze bandage. At first sign of chaffing put a piece of moleskin over the tender area. Change socks every few hours. See the Health and Care section on 'Foot Care.'

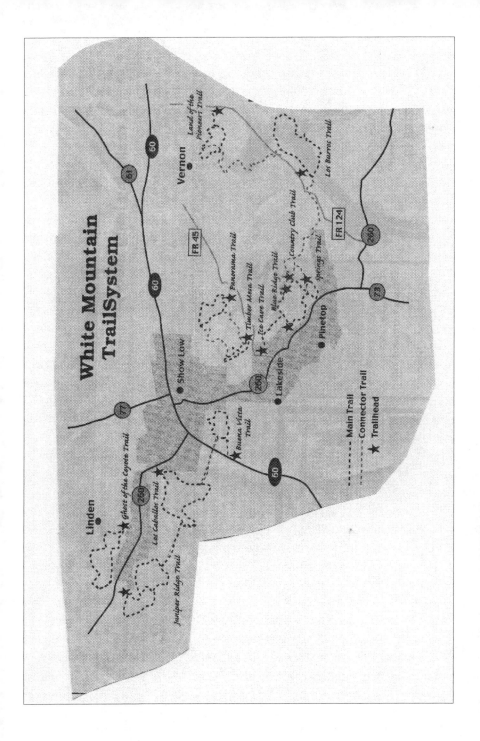

# White Mountain TrailSystem

Vernon

Land of the Pioneers Trail

Los Burros Trail

FR 124

Country Club Trail

Springs Trail

FR 45

Panorama Trail

Timber Mesa Trail

Ice Cave Trail

Blue Ridge Trail

Show Low

Pinetop

Lakeside

Buena Vista Trail

Linden

Ghost of the Coyote Trail

Los Cabalitos Trail

Juniper Ridge Trail

- - - - Main Trail
- - - - Connector Trail
★ Trailhead

# TRAIL DESCRIPTIONS IN THE FOLLOWING TOWNS

CLAY SPRINGS
LAKESIDE
LINDEN
PINEDALE

PINETOP
SHOW LOW
VERNON
(MCNARY)

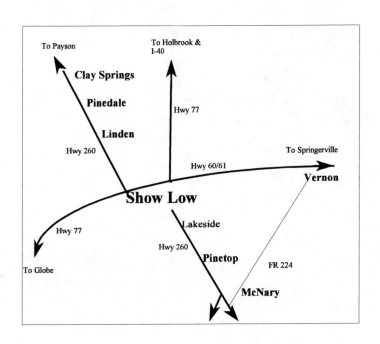

# CLAY SPRINGS

# One Way
## General Crook Trail #130
(The portion in Clay Springs & Pinedale.)

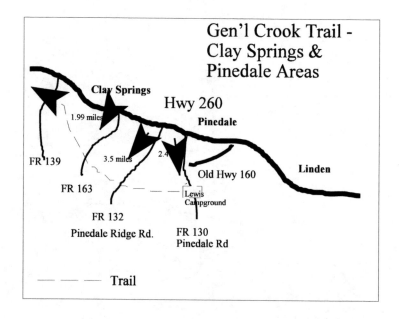

# NATIONAL RECREATION TRAIL & STATE HISTORIC TRAIL
# GENERAL CROOK TRAIL #130
# (CLAY SPRINGS, PINEDALE, & LINDEN)
# (One way)

*"Commit to the Lord whatever you do and your plans will succeed"*
*(Proverbs 16:3).*

LOCATION:  On the Mogollon Rim

LENGTH:  114 miles from historic Fort Verde (by the city of Camp
Verde) to west of the town Clay Springs.

In the mid-1860s trappers, prospectors, and settlers began to move into Central Arizona. The local Indians opposed the white man's intrusion and created problems. These problems were solved by bringing in the military and forcing the Yavapai and the Apache onto reservations.

An experienced and well-like commander called "Gray Wolf" by the Apache, Crook was one of the fairest officers to serve in Arizona. In order to accomplish his mission, he established a trail to move men and supplies across the rugged Mogollon rim country from Fort Whipple in the west to Fort Apache, his base of operations in the east.

His original trail was approximately 200 miles in length. General Crook recorded each mile by counting the revolutions of a wagon wheel and marking the trail with tree blazes and rock carvings at every milepost location. Telegraph lines between the forts were also strung along the route of the trail.

For 22 years the General Crook Trail was used by troops patrolling the northern portion of the Apache Indian territory. The trail follows one of the more striking geologic features in the state, the Mogollon Rim, and today's highways parallel this original trail. The General's last four years was spent trying to force the surrender of the Chiricahua leader, Geronimo. He was relieved of duty before that happened. Crook passed away in March of 1890.

After the surrender of the infamous Apache Indian leader, Geronimo, Arizonans continued to use the trail for travel until the completion of the highway in 1928, which totals 46 years of continuous trail usage. Today, Forest Road 300 parallels the trail much of the time and in some

27

places crosses or runs on top of the old trail. The trail itself has pretty much disappeared into FR 300 around the Show Low area heading south towards the Black River near Alpine.

Many miles of the state historic General Crook Trail are marked with rock cairns and white and yellow V-shaped chevrons that were placed on trees by the Boy Scouts of America. You can pick up the trail from the Lewis Campground in Pinedale and follow it westward.

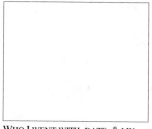

WHO I WENT WITH, DATE, & MY NOTES

USE: Light                                                           RATE: Hard

ACCESS AREAS OF HIGHWAY 260:
(A) Pinedale Road (FR 130) to the rear end of the Lewis Campground.
(B) Across the street from the Mormon Stake Center, Scotts Rd/Pinedale Ridge FR 132.
(C) Just past the town of Clay Springs on FR 139.

DIRECTIONS
(A) From the trailhead kiosk at the west end of Lewis Canyon Campground in Pinedale, follow the trail west, *past* the intersection for the Juniper Ridge Trail.
(B) To access the trail around its midpoint, continue on Hwy 260 to the Pinedale turnoff for about 2 miles. Turn left onto FR 132. After driving approximately 3.5 miles, look for blue diamonds on either side of the road. Finding a place to park is tough. You'll want to take the trail on the right side.
(C) From the gas station/ Victorian Bldg. Intersection (Hwys 60 & 260 in Show Low head west on Hwy 260 (towards Payson). The furthermost access point is 18.7 miles and will be on your left exactly half a mile pass the Cottonwood Wash sign. Parking is by the restroom building. You'll notice the Boy Scout's tree chevrons nailed to trees.

COMMENTS:   I haven't hiked the entire General Crook Trail at the time of writing this book. I put in an hour of walking westward from FR 139. Within these couple of miles, I found the trail to be level and easily walked marked with tree chevrons. A couple of weekends later I went back and looked for the trail going in the other direction (towards Pinedale) where it would end up at the Lewis Canyon Campground five plus miles later. If you plan on taking this connector trail from this point you'll have to scour around for it. Facing the restroom building from the highway walk to its immediate left and through the dilapidated fence. You should be able to spot a blue diamond in a few minutes.

*No trail map is provided. Refer to Rim Guide Hiking Map produced by Arizona Highways.*

# LAKESIDE

## Loop Trails
Panorama #635
Rim View #615
Timber Mesa #636

## One Way Trails
Ice Cave #608

## Connectors
The Flume #636b
   (Timber Mesa / Panorama)
The Sawmill #636a
   (Timber Mesa / Panorama)

# PANORAMA TRAIL #635 WOOLHOUSE WILDLIFE HABITAT AREA (Loop)

*"I have kept my feet from every evil path so that I might obey Your word" (Psalm 119:101).*

ATTRACTION: Panoramic Views
LOCATION: Lakeside

**The Walk**
LENGTH: 8.6 miles
RATE: Moderate
TIME: 4 hours

WHO I WENT WITH, DATE, & MY NOTES

DIRECTIONS: From Show Low head south to Lakeside on Hwy 260 (White Mountain Road). Turn left on Porter Mountain Road (FR 45) and travel six miles looking for FR 206 with a trailhead sign pointing to the trail.

USE: Infrequent                    PARKING: Plenty
DIRECTION TO TRAVEL: Counter-clockwise
ELEVATION RANGE: 7000' - 7100'

HIGHLIGHTS: Its been said that on a very clear day one can see the San Francisco Peaks in Flagstaff from the top of Twin Knolls. This trail passes through a portion of the Woolhouse Wildlife Habitat Area.

CONNECTOR TRAIL(S): Flume & Sawmill

MOUNTAIN(S): Porter and Twin Knolls

COMMENTS: I verified the mileage of this trail with a pedometer. It read the trail as 8.6 miles in length. After starting you'll soon come to a post with blue diamond and this is where the loop begins. I recommend going towards the right and proceeding counter-clockwise. Despite several shot up blue diamonds the trail is well marked until 3/4ths of the way through. You'll come out by Porter Tank (it was dry in April) and see a sign post. The sign reads to Timber Mesa and to South Tank. You just came from the South Tank direction, so be sure to take a left here.

It heads slightly uphill and you'll walk a bit before you see the next blue diamond. The hardest part of this trail was the initial climb up the narrow hill where you start getting great panoramic views. The day my husband, dogs, and I went, we spotted a large family of wild turkeys up the road. It was amazing that the dogs missed them!

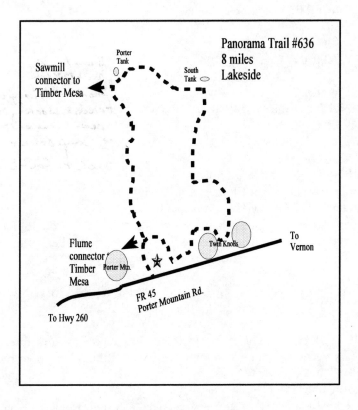

# RIM VIEW TRAIL #615 (OVERLOOK) (a.k.a. MONGOLLON RIM NATURE TRAIL) (Loop)

*"And He is not served by human hands, as if He needed anything, because He Himself gives all men life and breath and everything else" (Acts 17:25).*

ATTRACTION: Panoramic views of the rim, self-guided & wheelchair accessible.

LOCATION: Lakeside

**The Walk**
LENGTH: 1 mile
RATE: Easy
TIME: 30 minutes

June 1, C4
Me + Morgan
Short hike-Logging
trucks working in
area- Came out
@ Camp Grace +
back to Car-Some photos

WHO I WENT WITH, DATE, & MY NOTES

DIRECTIONS: From Show Low Post Office, take Deuce of Clubs east to White Mountain Lake Road (Hwy 260) and head south half a mile past the highway marker 347; look for the Rim Trail sign between the signs for Camp Grace and Camp Tatihee. A Smokey the Bear sign also marks the entrance.

USE: Very heavy
DIRECTION TO TRAVEL: Clockwise
PARKING: Plenty
ELEVATION: 6,800 feet

DESCRIPTION: This rather level trail affords the most picturesque and excellent panoramic view of the Mogollon Rim. It is an interpretive trail with 16 descriptive signs giving history, plants, and animal information. Pacific willow and Bebb's willow, together with a wide variety of water plants and sedges can be found growing along an irrigation ditch which has an interesting history relating to pioneers in the area. More kinds of trees, bushes, and shrubs can be seen growing side by side along this trail than any other in this area.

HISTORY: This trail used to be called the "Mogollon Rim Overlook". Named after a mid-1700 Spanish Governor of the Province of New Mexico (1712-15), Don Juan Ignacio Flores Mogollon, of this territory, it attracts thousands of visitors per year and is a nature trail identifying and interpreting the area's valuable resources. An excellent view of the valley below the Mogollon Rim is located at a sandstone rock outcrop. Excellent photo opportunities exist.

Forest Road 300 (a.k.a. Rim Road & General Crook Trail) cuts through part of this trail. This part of the General Crook Trail is really the forest road, and I don't consider it a trail. The real trail can be picked up in Linden at the Juniper Ridge Trail or just past Clay Springs.

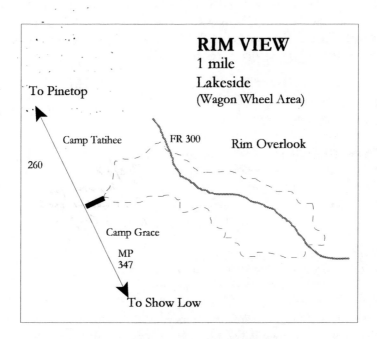

COMMENT: The book's title, Walking the Edge, came from this trail's breathtakingly view overlooking the rim and the General Crook trail which follows the edge for miles.

# TIMBER MESA TRAIL #636 (Loop)

*"Man looks on the outward appearance, but God looks on the heart"*
*(1 Samuel 16:7).*

ATTRACTION: Panoramic views          LOCATION: Lakeside

**The Walk**
LENGTH: 6 miles                              RATE: Easy
TIME: 2 ½ hours

DIRECTIONS: From Show Low head south on Hwy 260 to Lakeside. Turn left on Porter Mountain Road (FR #45) (just past the Lakeside Ranger Station). Follow for 2.2 miles. Take a left at the cattle guard and continue a short distance to the trailhead.

USE: Mild                                          PARKING: Plenty
DIRECTION TO TRAVEL: Counter-clockwise
ELEVATION: 6640' - 6960'

DESCRIPTION: The loop trail follows the top edge of the mesa and loops back along the Chimneys Fire Road. The trail on top of the mesa is rocky. From the top of the mesa you'll be able to make out the town of Pinetop-Lakeside, as well as the wetland marsh / wildlife habitat called Jacques Marsh. Keep your eyes open for remnants of a cabin. The tank near it is called the Sawmill Tank. For some more hiking fun, see if you can spot the Bureau of Land Management's survey monument T9NR22E with its nearby bearing trees. Pay particular attention to following the blue diamonds when you get down off the top because of several dissecting dirt roads.

7/8/06
Me + Morgan
Trail head / Creek
Photo Trip -

WHO I WENT WITH, DATE, & MY NOTES

CONNECTOR TRAIL(S): Flume & Sawmill

COMMENTS: There are plans to make a connector trail between Timber Mesa and Ice Cave trails in the year 2003.

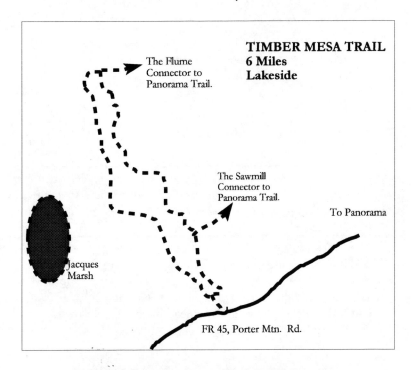

The Flume Connector to Panorama Trail.

**TIMBER MESA TRAIL
6 Miles
Lakeside**

The Sawmill Connector to Panorama Trail.

To Panorama

Jacques Marsh

FR 45, Porter Mtn. Rd.

# ICE CAVE TRAIL #608 (a.k.a. BLUE RIDGE CAVE TRAIL) (One way)

*"He set the earth on its foundations; it can never be moved" (Psalm 104:5).*

ATTRACTION: Stream & lake

LOCATION: Lakeside

**The Walk**
LENGTH: 3.5 miles (one way)
RATE: Moderate

TIME: 3 hours (round trip)

> **NOTE**: At the time of this writing, the cave has been fenced off for its protection and preservation and the trail has been re-routed past the ice cave and connects to the Blue Ridge loop trail. There is an extension path to the ice cave.

DIRECTIONS: From Show Low's post office head 1 mile east on the Deuce of Clubs to White Mountain Road and make a right. Head south 8.85 miles to Lakeside, turning left on Porter Mountain Road. Follow this road (FR 45) for 1 mile. The trailhead is on the right opposite the Humane Society's sign.

USE: Moderate

PARKING: Plenty

ELEVATION RANGE: 6,900 to 7,200 feet

DESCRIPTION: The trail winds its way along Porter Creek and the south side of Scott Reservoir and now leads directly to the Blue Ridge Trail. The trail is very rocky and frequently muddy in areas with large pot holes created by cattle. From the trailhead hikers can experience a riparian environment along Porter Creek and Scott Reservoir before heading up to higher elevations. Along the way one can see wild flowers such as sego lilly, fleabane daisy, sennicio or groundsel, yellow salsify, stinging nettle, Indian paintbrush, purple bush penstemon, and rocky mountain juniper, and Utah juniper. Some shrubs in the area include skunk bush, gooseberry currant, wild currant, and willows. Other plants to see include wild parsley, prickly pear cactus, penny cress, pussy toes, wild grape, golden pea, and many common water plants. Although chances are good you will encounter cows, you may also notice a variety of birds and the occasional deer or elk.

COMMENTS: The Blue Ridge Cave is not spectacular and due to vandalism and safety reasons has not only been fenced and locked, but the trail has been rerouted away from and past it. If you keep alert you may notice a rock cairn that marks the short 500' extension to the cave. Literature on the cave states that a trail to it was first marked by a group of local Boy Scouts about 1920. The cave itself consists of an entry room, largely filled in with debris; a rather large second room, and a third room that can only be reached by crawling on hands and knees. This third room is quite small; just barely enough to stand and move around. It is thought that its entrance came about from a "cave-in" (no pun intended) or that it was a lava tube that drained and formed a hollow tunnel. I do not know how it came by the name 'Ice' cave, other than guessing the consistent air temperature of the cave is a cool 52 degrees.

WHO I WENT WITH, DATE, & MY NOTES

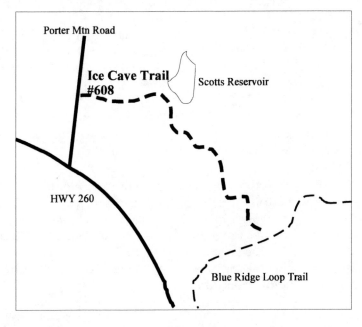

Porter Mtn Road

Ice Cave Trail
#608

Scotts Reservoir

HWY 260

Blue Ridge Loop Trail

# THE FLUME "CONNECTOR" TRAIL
## #636b (PANORAMA TO TIMBER MESA) (One way)

*"Blessed is the man who does not walk in the counsel of the wicked or stand in the way of sinners or sit in the seat of mockers" (Psalm 1:1).*

LOCATION:  Lakeside

**The Walk**
LENGTH: 2.5 miles (one way)
RATE:  Moderate
TIME:  1 ½ hours (one way)

WHO I WENT WITH, DATE, & MY NOTES

DIRECTIONS:  From Show Low head to Lakeside on Hwy 260 and turn left on Porter Mountain Road (FR 45) for 2.2 miles. Take a left at the cattle guard for Timber Mesa Trailhead or continue on Porter Mountain Road for 3.8 miles to Panorama Trailhead.

USE:  Infrequent                                           PARKING:  Plenty
ELEVATION RANGE:  6900' - 7120'

TRAIL DIRECTIONS TO THE FLUME:  From the Timber Mesa Trailhead walk counter clockwise. Follow the trail approximately 15 minutes up to the blue diamond with 2 green dots/636b which veers off to the right. It is a well marked connector trail.

HIGHLIGHTS:  This is called the Flume Connector trail because it is named for the irrigation pipe that is visible on the south side of FR 45 just east of the Timber Mesa Trailhead turnoff.

COMMENTS:  If you plan on hiking just this trail, please allow 2 ½ to 3 hours. My husband, three dogs, and I started at 2:15 pm and finished at 4:55 pm, 2 ½ hours, with a 20 minute break. However, we power walked it, so I would add more time to your schedule so that you can enjoy the scenery and go at a leisurely pace. In starting off on this trail you will go up the hill and can see across to Jacques Marsh, the parking area and the nearby residential area.

# THE SAWMILL "CONNECTOR" #636a
# (TIMBER MESA TO PANORAMA)
# (One way)

*"By faith we understand that the universe was formed at God's command, so that what is seen was not made out of what was visible" (Hebrews 11:3).*

LOCATION: Lakeside

**The Walk**
LENGTH: 4 miles (one way)
RATE: Moderate
TIME: 2 hours (round trip)

WHO I WENT WITH, DATE, & MY NOTES

DIRECTIONS: From Show Low head to Lakeside and just past the Lakeside Ranger Station make a left on Porter Mountain Road. Follow this road for 2.2 miles. Take a left at the cattle guard for Timber Mesa Trailhead or continue on Porter Mtn. Road for 3.8 miles to the Panorama Trailhead.

USE: Little                                     PARKING: Plenty
DIRECTION TO TRAVEL: From Timber Mesa east to Panorama.
ELEVATION RANGE: 6720' - 6920'

MOUNTAIN: Porter

TRAIL DIRECTIONS TO THE FLUME: From the Timber Mesa Trailhead go either direction as this connector is pretty much at the half-way point. It is marked with a sign.

COMMENTS: The hiker should take into consideration the additional time it takes to 'reach' and 'return' from the trail she or he is taking to reach the connector.

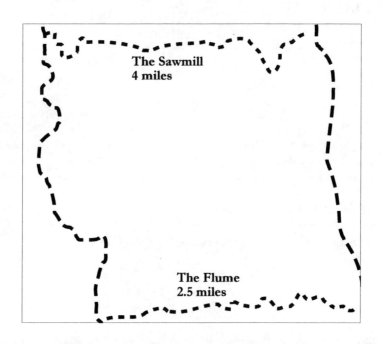

The Sawmill
4 miles

The Flume
2.5 miles

Candy, Pepsi, Popcorn ready to go.

# LINDEN

## Loop Trails
Ghost of the Coyote #641
Los Caballos #638

## Connectors
The Chihuahua Pine #638a
   (Los Caballos / Buena Vista)

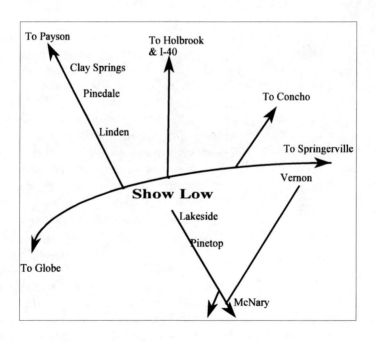

# GHOST OF THE COYOTE TRAIL #641
(Loop)

*"Be still and know that I am God" (Psalm 46:10).*

ATTRACTION: Panoramic views          LOCATION: Linden

**The Walk**
LENGTH: 16 miles                              RATE: Hard

DIRECTIONS: From the Show Low Post Office turn left on the Deuce of Clubs and follow to Hwy. 260 west (toward Payson). Drive for 8.1 miles making a right on Burton Road and going 1.1 miles to the trailhead on the left.

USE: Little                                        PARKING: Plenty
ELEVATION RANGE: 6300' - 6700'
DIRECTION TRAVELED: Counter-clockwise

DESCRIPTION: The trail follows portions of old logging roads through pinon-juniper forest. Views of the White Mountains can be seen. Wildlife is abundant in this area to include javelina and turkey. It is best to take this trail in cooler weather as its out in the open.

WHO I WENT WITH, DATE, & MY NOTES

HISTORY: In the distant past, indigenous peoples were apparently fond of this area. There are several sites in the area where evidence of past occupation may be found such as pottery shards, stone tools, and the foundations of dwellings. Federal law prohibits the excavation or removal of artifacts form these sites. Each site is like a history book that has yet to even be opened. It is a record of animals, events and people that have passed over the place. <u>Please do not remove any objects.</u>

COMMENTS: Keep your eyes and ears open for coyotes. This very adaptive predator plays an important role in nature's ecosystem. While they eat anything from insects to an elk carcass, they primarily prey on small rodents. As hunters, they depend on their acute senses, exceptional speed (40 mph) and leaping ability (10 feet). These cunning animals rival a cat in stalking ability.

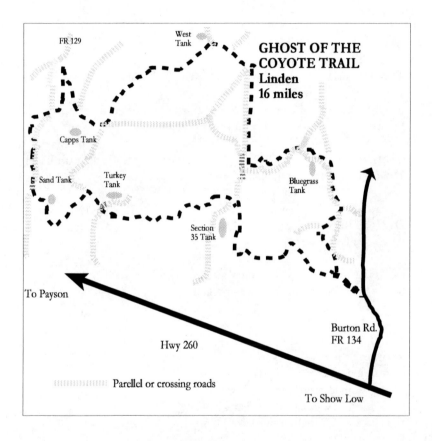

COMMENTS: Although the above map doesn't show it, short cut(s) were established on this trail. Blue diamonds with <u>yellow</u> dots indicate a short cut. You'll also notice the damage done by the 2002 Rodeo-Chediski fire.

# LOS CABALLOS TRAIL #638 (Loop)

*"I the Lord search the heart, I try the reins, even to give every man according to his ways, and according to the fruit of his doings" (Jeremiah 17:10).*

LOCATION: Linden

**The Walk**
LENGTH: 14+ miles                             RATE: Hard
TIME: 8 hours

DIRECTIONS: From the Show Low Post Office turn left on the Deuce of Clubs and then right on Hwy 260 (towards Payson). Follow Hwy 260 for 3.9 miles, (just past Bison Ranch entrance) and making a *sharp* left on FR 136 (unmarked, but often called Joe Tank Farm Road). The trail-head is 0.6 mile ahead on the right.

USE: Mild                                          PARKING: Plenty
DIRECTION TRAVELED: Clockwise
ELEVATION RANGE: 6350' - 6940'

HIGHLIGHTS: Los Caballos means "the horses" in Spanish and is rugged with a few short steep grades to climb. It is a beautiful trail encompassing a sampling of trees and flora this area has to offer. It is one of the longest trails mentioned in this book. The majority of the trail follows old logging roads and winds its way along Joe Tank ridge and through Bagnal Draw. Take plenty of water with you. You'll see three tanks, but by far the prettiest one is in a park like setting about halfway along your journey. At a distance it looks like a lake. The berm around it is actually

WHO I WENT WITH, DATE, & MY NOTES

part of the trail. Nearby is the largest pine tree ever seen. Best scenic views are about five miles out when you're hiking along side a ridge and can see as far as the distant snow covered mountains and realize there are absolutely no signs of human civilization around. You'll notice about five wooden trail signs, but not a single one calling out how many miles left to go. On a long trail like this, you are going to wish you knew! Connector trail signs are extremely hard to find.

CONNECTOR TRAILS: The 'Chihuahua Pine' trail connects to Buena Vista and is approximately four miles. The 'Lookout' Trail connects to the Juniper Ridge Trail which is approximately two and half miles. (Mileage given by Beth Purchell of the Lakeside Forest District Office.) See respective listed trails by these names.

SHORT CUTS: See the trail drawing and take one of the forest roads back towards the trailhead.

COMMENTS: Per 02/29/00 phone call to Pinetop-Lakeside Parks & Recreation Dept., Dave Matthews told me that this trail is closer to 17 miles in length.

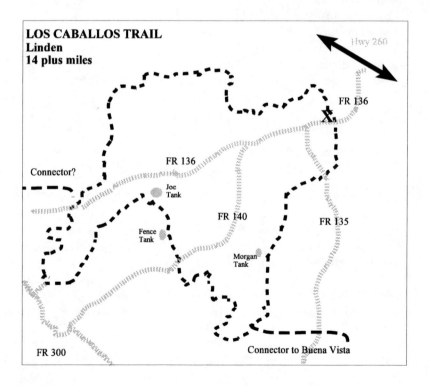

LOS CABALLOS TRAIL
Linden
14 plus miles

Hwy 260

FR 136

Connector?

FR 136

Joe
Tank

FR 140

FR 135

Fence
Tank

Morgan
Tank

FR 300

Connector to Buena Vista

# THE CHIHUAHUA PINE "CONNECTOR" TRAIL #638a (LOS CABALLOS TO BUENA VISTA) (One way)

*"If we confess our sins, He is faithful and just and will forgive us our sins and purify us from all unrighteousness" (1 John 1:9).*

LOCATION: Linden to Show Low

**The Walk**
LENGTH: 4.5 miles (one way)
RATE: Hard
TIME: 2.5 hrs

LOS CABALLOS DIRECTIONS: From the corner of the gas station & Victorian Building (Hwys 60, 77, 260 intersection) head 2.8 miles on Hwy 77 in the direction of Globe. Turn left on FR 300 and the trailhead is on your immediate left.

WHO I WENT WITH, DATE, & MY NOTES

BUENA VISTA DIRECTIONS: From the corner of the gas station & Victorian Building (Hwys 60, 77, 260 intersection) head 2.8 miles on Hwy 77 in the direction of Globe. Turn left on FR 300 and the trailhead is on your immediate left. Plenty of parking is available.

USE: Infrequent                    PARKING: Plenty

SUGGESTED HIKING DIRECTION : Buena Vista towards Los Caballos. (Easier and quicker to reach the connector trail.) Follow directions to this connector trail as given on page 79.

COMMENTS: This trail was completed in the summer of 1999. It is rated hard because of several steep climbs and rocky terrain.

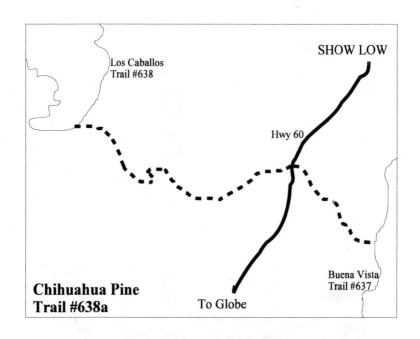

**Chihuahua Pine**
**Trail #638a**

Los Caballos
Trail #638

SHOW LOW

Hwy 60

To Globe

Buena Vista
Trail #637

# PINEDALE

## Loop Trails
Juniper Ridge #640

## Connectors
Juniper Ridge/Gen'l Crook
The Lookout #640a
    (Juniper Ridge / Los Caballos)

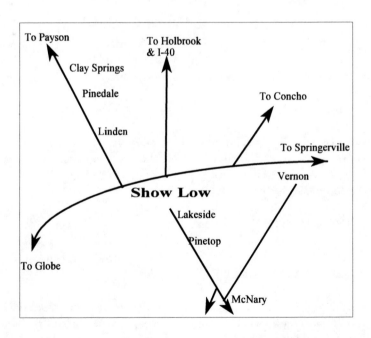

# JUNIPER RIDGE TRAIL #640 (Loop)

*"All discipline for the moment seems not to be joyful, but sorrowful; yet to those who have been trained by it, afterwards it yields the peaceful fruit of righteousness"*
*(Hebrews 12:11).*

ATTRACTION:  Views & Look Out Tower

LOCATION:  Pinedale

**The Walk**
DISTANCE:  14 miles
TIME:  8 hours
RATE:  Hard

ELEVATION RANGE:  6400' - 7000'

WHO I WENT WITH, DATE, &
MY NOTES

DIRECTION TRAVELED:  Counter-clockwise

DIRECTIONS:  From the Show Low Post Office, travel west on Hwy. 260 (corner of the gas station & Victorian building). Follow for 11 miles to Farnsworth Ranch Road (a.k.a. Old Highway 160). Turn left and the trailhead is two miles on the right.

PARKING:  Plenty                                              USE:  Little

DESCRIPTION:  This trail winds through the manzanita-pine country. There is a short loop cutting the trail roughly in half. It is best to hike this trail in cool weather. At its height the trail cuts across the Juniper Ridge Look Out Tower.

LOOK OUT TOWER:  Juniper Ridge Look Out Tower

SHORT LOOP:  The short cut bypasses the tower and cuts the distance down to approximately 7.2 miles.

CONNECTOR TRAIL(S):  One leads to the Gen'l Crook trail when you get into the Lewis Canyon Campground. One leads to the Los Caballos trail. See their descriptions in this book.

**CAUTION:** The Rodeo-Chediski Fire of 2002 (see page 144) did serious damage to this area and most of the blue diamonds were destroyed. The TRACKS organization will make repairs in the future.

REMINDER: Yellow dots attached to the blue diamonds indicate you are on a short loop. Green circles signify a connector trail. As with all the trails mentioned in this and other books, keep alert for the trail markers. It is very easy to overlook them. With all of the logging roads and other paths dissecting trails you must continuously be aware that you are following the marked trail. On this particular trail, it will be very easy to keep walking down a wide path, just to end up back-tracking because the trail had veered off and you missed seeing the blue diamond. You may want to consider allowing extra time to hike this trail.

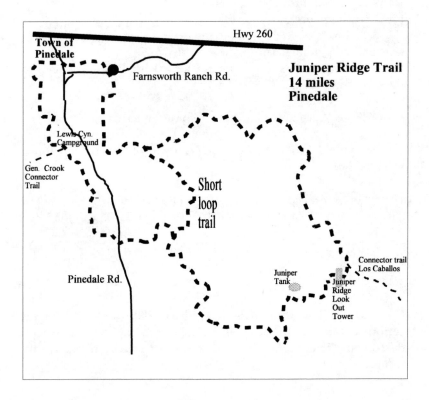

*Logging roads are not shown on map.*

# JUNIPER RIDGE TO GENERAL CROOK "CONNECTOR" TRAIL (One way)

*"Hallelujah! Salvation and glory and power belong to our God"*
*(Revelation 19:1b).*

LOCATION:  Pinedale to Clay Springs

**The Walk**
DISTANCE:  5 miles +/- (one way)
TIME:  2 ½ hrs
RATE:  Easy

DIRECTIONS:  From Show Low head west
towards Payson on Hwy 260. Take a left on
Pinedale Road and go 2.4 miles to the Lewis
Canyon Campground. Turn right and drive to
WHO I WENT WITH, DATE,
& MY NOTES
the rear of the campground to the trailhead. Park. Follow the signs to
the General Crook Trail.

PARKING:  A fee might be assessed for using the campground.

DIRECTION TO TRAVEL:  At the rear part of Lewis Campground
you'll find the trail sign.

USE:  Undetermined          ELEVATION RANGE:  6400' - 7000'
TRAIL MAP:  See previous page 'Juniper Ridge Trail' map for
location.

*A complete map of this trail is not included.*

**CAUTION:  The Rodeo-Chediski Fire of 2002 (see page 144) did
serious damage to this area and most of the blue diamonds were
destroyed.  The TRACKS organization will make repairs in the
future.**

# THE LOOKOUT "CONNECTOR" TRAIL
# #640a (JUNIPER RIDGE TO LOS CABALLOS)(One way)

*"For though we walk in the flesh, we do not war according to the flesh, for the weapons of our warfare are not of the flesh, but divinely powerful for the destruction of fortresses" (2 Corinthians 10:3).*

LOCATION: Pinedale to Linden

**The Walk**
DISTANCE: 3.5 miles (one way)
TIME: 4 hours PLUS round trip

DIRECTIONS: The most direct way to this connector trail would be to drive up to Juniper Ridge lookout tower. Follow Hwy 260 west toward Pinedale until you reach Farnsworth Ranch Road (a.k.a. Old Hwy. 160). Turn left on Farnsworth Ranch Road and follow for 1 ½ miles looking for the lookout tower sign. Turn left and follow this rough dirt road for four miles up to the tower. Park at the tower and looking to its left; you'll walk through a gate and after a few steps you'll see the green dots on a blue diamond indicating this connector trail.

WHO I WENT WITH, DATE, & MY NOTES

PARKING: Limited                    USE: Infrequent

DIRECTION TO TRAVEL: Juniper Ridge to Los Caballos. Going this direction will be heading downward.

ELEVATION: 6,998 ft.                    RATE: Moderate

COMMENTS: In October 2000, my hubby (Al) and dogs decided to walk this connector. We took both of our vehicles. We parked one car down on FR 136 (Joe Tank Rd.) at the point where the Los Caballos trail crosses the road. This point is 3.8 miles down FR 136, pass FR 135 and FR 140. Then together we drove the other vehicle over and up to the Juniper Ridge lookout tower. We had every intention of hiking this connector ending up where we'd left the first car, and then car pooling back to the lookout tower for the other vehicle. However, from the tower we could see a huge storm which had risen up over the rim in the ½ hour since we had dropped off the truck. The black sky totally covered the distance of the direction we were going to take. It looked like a huge thunderstorm and it changed our plans. Needless to say we did only a very small part of this hike before having to backtrack and give up. The factual information on this trail has been gleaned from public sources. I suspect this trail is longer than 3 ½ miles if one was to hike it in its entirety.

HISTORY: Completed by the Lakeside Forest Service during the summer of 1999.

COMMENTS: Mileage and trail number taken from the White Mountain Independent Newspaper, dated Tuesday, March 28, 2000, 'Progress of Our White Mountain Trails', page 10B, para. 2.

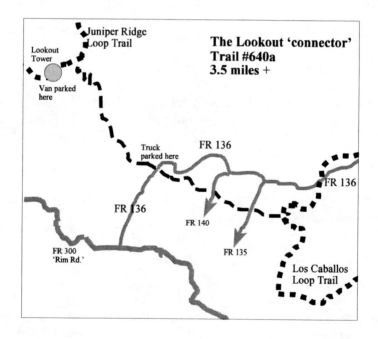

# PINETOP

## Loop Trails
Blue Ridge #107
Country Club #632
Laurie's Delight
Springs #633
Woodland Lake Park Trails

## One Way Trails
Old Hatchery

## Connector Trails
Iron Horse #632a
    (Country Club / Springs)

## Access Trails
Pinecrest (Billy Creek Trails Park)

# BLUE RIDGE TRAIL #107 (Loop)

*"Prepare a road for the Lord - straighten out the path where He will walk"*
*(Matthew 3:3b).*

ATTRACTION:  Scenic views

LOCATION:  Pinetop

**The Walk**
DISTANCE:  8.7 miles
TIME:  3.5 to 4 hours
DIRECTION TO TRAVEL:  Clockwise

WHO I WENT WITH, DATE, & MY NOTES

DIRECTIONS ~ **Trailhead #1**: From Show Low's post office, take the Deuce of Clubs east and turn right onto White Mountain Road (Hwy 260). Travel south on Hwy. 260 to Pinetop. Make a left turn (north) at the Baptist Church & Pet Clinic (Moonridge Drive), travel north .3 mile and turn right on Billy Creek. Follow this road east 0.3 mile and make a sharp left on Meadow Dr. You'll cross Billy Creek Bridge. Follow the road as it turns right and is called Pine Shadow Drive. Continue to follow up the hill (becomes Springer Mtn. Drive). At the top of the hill (.8 mile), turn right at FR 187, cross the cattle guard, you will see a water tank to the right. Stay on FR 187 for 0.7 miles until you come to the trailhead parking lot. You'll past the turnoff for Springer Mountain Look Out Tower along the way. **Trailhead #2:** From Show Low travel south (Hwy 260 White Mountain Rd) to Pinetop. Turn left (east) on Bucksprings Road; Left (north) on Sky High Road (FR 182); and left (west) on FR 187 to Trailhead #2. You can continue on FR 187 to reach Trailhead #1. Be aware that the roads are unimproved and quite rough.

RATE: Moderate                                              USE: Popular
ELEVATION:  7100' to 7656'                     PARKING: Limited

DESCRIPTION:  Small portions of the trail follow old logging roads. Pay careful attention to the blue diamonds because of the old roads that traverse the trails at times. In particular, pay attention to the blue diamonds when you near Blue Ridge Mountain because the trail turns off while the logging road keeps going straight. The grade varies from level ground to 10 percent grade. Parts of the trail are quite rough due to the volcanic origin of the area. It follows Billy Creek and winds its way through the pine tree forest to the top of Blue Ridge Mountain. The mountain is volcanic in origin and the trail takes you up near the top where you can see vistas of the forest, towns, and roadways. Indian paintbrush, penstemon, oxeye daisy, aster, and gilia bloom during various times of the year. Wild rose, willow, and clover shade the banks of Billy Creek. Blue Ridge Mountain is volcanic in origin and is one of the major geological features in this area. As the trail leads down the east side of Blue Ridge Mountain, there are a few rather remarkable views of the Mount Baldy region.

As you walk look for stands of white barked, quaking aspen trees. Listen... can you hear them "quake"? A very slight breeze causes the leaves to rustle creating shimmering sounds similar to a small brook. This special quality is primarily due to the flat, rather than tubular, construction of the petiole (stem) which catches the wind and is much more flexible than the common tubular shape, thus allowing the leaves to rustle much more easily. Aspens commonly grow closely together in stands. New trees sprout from the roots of older trees, particularly following a forest fire. Aspens rarely grow older than 200 years of age and actually begin to deteriorate just after 80 years.

CONNECTOR TRAIL(S): One heads southeast to the Springs Loop Trail, one northwest to the Ice Cave Trail, and one west to Billy Creek Trails Park (Pinecrest).

MOUNTAIN(S): Blue Ridge

SHORT CUT: You can always cut some distance off by walking down FR 187 back to either trailhead.

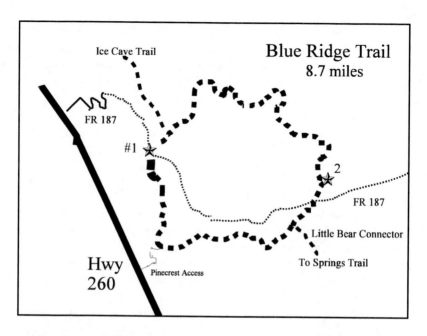

**Blue Ridge Trail**
8.7 miles

Ice Cave Trail

FR 187

#1

2

FR 187

Little Bear Connector

To Springs Trail

Hwy
260

Pinecrest Access

# COUNTRY CLUB TRAIL #632 (Loop)

*"For the invisible things of Him from the creation of the world are clearly seen, being understood by the things that are made, even His eternal power and Godhead; so that they are without excuse" (Romans 1:20).*

LOCATION: Pinetop

**The Walk**
DISTANCE: 3.5 miles
TIME: 1 ½ hrs          RATE: Easy
DIRECTION TRAVELED: Counter-clockwise

DIRECTIONS: From Show Low head south on AZ 260 (White Mountain Rd) and turn left on Bucksprings Road (right outside the town of Pinetop). Travel half a mile and turn left on Sky High Road (FR 182). The trailhead is two miles ahead on the right at the junction of FR 185. You'll see a sign for Sierra Springs Drive.

WHO I WENT WITH, DATE, & MY NOTES

PARKING: Plenty          ELEVATION: 7200', level
USE: Moderate

DESCRIPTION: This trail loops through the forest and follows portions of an old railroad bed used in the turn of the century for transporting timber products. The trailhead starts you off going counterclockwise.

CONNECTOR TRAIL(S): One leads to Springs #633 and another to Los Burros #631. You will see two different signs along the way for connecting to Los Burros, they each say 7 miles. Both Springs and Los Burros connector trails are described under their own heading.

SPUR TRAIL: A ½ mile spur trail (Vista View) leads to the top of Pat Mullen Mountain (elevation 7612'). (My friend, Dick Williams, who loves hiking, said that when he got to the top of this spur there was a sign calling it McKay point.)

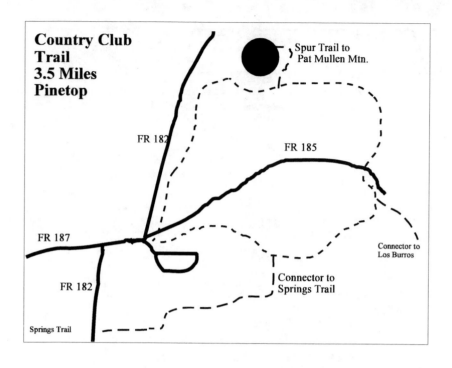

**Country Club Trail 3.5 Miles Pinetop**

Spur Trail to Pat Mullen Mtn.

FR 182

FR 185

FR 187

Connector to Los Burros

FR 182

Connector to Springs Trail

Springs Trail

*Secondary fire or logging roads do intersect this trail, but are not shown on this map.*

# LAURIE'S DELIGHT, Billy Creek Trails Park (Loop)

*"Within Your temple, O God, we meditate on Your unfailing love"*
*(Psalm 48:9).*

ATTRACTION: Riparian environment, multiple trails

LOCATION: Pinetop

DIRECTIONS: From Show Low head south on White Mountain Road (Hwy 260) to Lakeside, turn left at the Best Western Inn of Pinetop (Pinecrest Avenue) and follow short distance and park at the dead end. There is a forest service "V" walk-through. Trailhead indicates the trail as being Blue Ridge Trail #107.

WHO I WENT WITH, DATE, & MY NOTES

**The Walk**
DISTANCE: 1.59 miles              TIME: 45 minutes
DIRECTION TO TRAVEL: Clockwise

TRAIL ROUTE: From the "v" walk-through, follow the marked trail for Blue Ridge veering to the left at the "T". Follow the trail down and alongside the creek. In less than a mile (.89) the path will come to the creek where you will naturally want to cross. **DON'T!** Instead, take a sharp right and head the short distance up the slight grade. This leads to the wide dirt path that will take you back around. Follow it to the brown hiker's sign which will lead you slightly towards the right. By following this path you will shortly end up back at the trailhead where you started.

PARKING: Very limited          ELEVATION: 6,940 - 7,026 ft.
USE: Popular                   RATE: Easy

COMMENTS: This trail is named after the author and isn't an 'official' trail. It lends itself beautifully as a 'get away' from crowds to enjoy a leisurely shaded stroll. *No trail map provided.*

# SPRINGS TRAIL #633 (a.k.a. THOMPSON SPRING AREA) (Loop)

*"When I consider Your heavens, the work of Your fingers, the moon and the stars, which You have set in place, what is man that You are mindful of him, the son of man that You care for him? (Psalm 8: 3,4).*

ATTRACTION: Riparian                    LOCATION: Pinetop

**The Walk**
LENGTH: 3.8 miles                    RATE: Easy
TIME: 1 hour 35 minutes at fast pace

DIRECTIONS: Head south on White Mtn. Road to Pinetop (12.35 miles from Show Low's post office). Turn left on Buck Springs Road, follow ½ mile, then left again on Sky High Road (FR 182). Continue 1.1 miles to the trailhead (left side).

USE: Very popular                    PARKING: Plenty
DIRECTION TO TRAVEL: Counter clockwise
ELEVATION: 7100' - 7200'

DESCRIPTION: The Springs Trail is a relatively level hike that will take you along part of Billy Creek and Thompson Creek riparian areas. It is best to go when it hasn't recently rained as this trail can get very muddy. It is a popular trail for horseback riders and cyclists.

WHO I WENT WITH, DATE, & MY NOTES

CONNECTOR TRAIL(S): <u>Little Bear to Blue Ridge Trail</u>. This short (.2) connector trail is called by this name at the Springs Trailhead and rarely mentioned in other publications by name because it is so short. <u>Old Hatchery Bridge Trail</u> (half a mile to bridge and .2 further to Hwy 260 near the AZ Fish & Game Dept.) I have included a more lengthy description in this book. See Old Hatchery Trail on page 70.

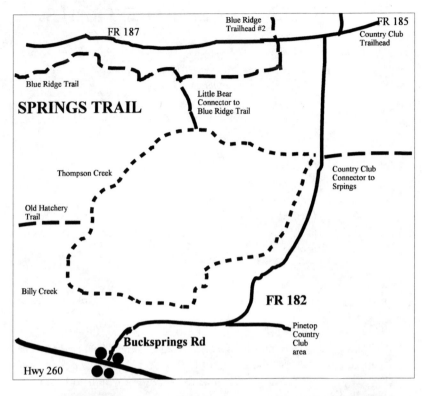

FR 187

Blue Ridge Trailhead #2

FR 185

Country Club Trailhead

Blue Ridge Trail

# SPRINGS TRAIL

Little Bear Connector to Blue Ridge Trail

Thompson Creek

Country Club Connector to Srpings

Old Hatchery Trail

Billy Creek

FR 182

Buucksprings Rd

Pinetop Country Club area

Hwy 260

# WOODLAND LAKE PARK TRAILS

*"Walk in all the way that the LORD your God has commanded you, so that you may live and prosper and prolong your days in the land that you will possess"*
*(Deuteronomy 5:33).*

ATTRACTION:  The lake and a pleasing combination of forest, lake, stream, wildlife, and recreation.

LOCATION:  Pinetop

**The Walks**
LAKE WALK (Loop)
Paved, 1.25 miles                                     Time:  40 minutes
Wheelchair accessible

HITCHING POST (Loop)
Wide dirt path, 2 miles                        Time:  1 hour 15 minutes

NOTE:  The path to Hitching Post loop is unnamed. One may reach Hitching Post Loop from Meadowview, Big Springs, Turkey Track, or this unnamed trail. The latter starts from the Lake Walk paved trail. Accessed from the far western half of the lake walk, you'll add a mile to your walk. See map.

MEADOW VIEW (One way) A .29 wide dirt rock-lined path leading from the parking lot to Hitching Post Loop. When taking this trail as a connector to Hitching Post, and the trail ends at a 'T' intersection, turn right and follow .43 to Hitching Post. Turning left takes you to the western side of Woodland Lake.

TURKEY TRACK (One way) Wide dirt path, approx. one mile.
Time:  30 minutes one way

WALNUT CREEK (One way) (a.k.a. Walnut Springs Nature Trail). Narrow, rocky, and wet path, approx. ½ mile in length. Time:  30 minutes one way

DIRECTIONS: From the Show Low intersection of Deuce of Clubs and White Mountain Road head south 260 to the town of Pinetop. At approximately 11 miles you'll turn right on Woodland Lake Road (gas station on corner). Follow this road to the park's *first* entrance (on your right). Follow this road to its end (boat dock) and park. Trails start here. All the trails are easy.

USE: Moderate
PARKING: Plenty all around the park
RATED: All trails rated easy.
ELEVATION: 6,950 feet.

WHO I WENT WITH, DATE, & MY NOTES .

HISTORY: Woodland Lake Park is at the heart of the 200 mile long White Mountain Trail System, planned and executed by volunteers for the purpose of keeping Pinetop-Lakeside residents connected to the national forest. The park is in use year around. The community uses the park for athletic activities when the weather permits. The town has built tennis courts, volleyball courts, softball fields, soccer fields, ramadas for family picnics, rest rooms, charcoal grills, and a boat dock. In addition, there are benches placed at intervals on the trails where people may sit and rest, and enjoy the sunset.

The Walnut Creek area was first developed as a nature trail in 1967 at the beginning of the Forest Service's Visitor Information Program. It gets its name from several small springs bubbling from the east side of the creek and the black walnut trees that are part of a favorite habitat of birds and squirrels. Between 80 and 100 trees, shrubs, grasses, and flowers have been identified along the creek.

*Look for Witch Brooms.* This is the nick name for perverted tree branches which show knarly growth as a response to the damage mistletoe has inflicted upon it.

*Look for Lichen.* Lichen grows on rocks and is a combination of fungi and algae. Fungi and algae have a symbiotic relationship where one can't live without the other. Fungi lack chlorophyll and are unable to make their own food.

CONNECTOR PATHWAYS (all short paths)
To *Big Springs Environmental Study Area*, found at north tip of Hitching Post Loop.
To *Turkey Track & Adair Streets*, found off of Turkey Track Trail.
To *Pinecrest Road*, found off Turkey Track Trail.

## A Day in Woodland Park

The day my friend, Pat, and I with my three dogs, walked these trails, we were checking out how accurate the Park & Rec's park handout was. Our overall thoughts were that the handout wasn't precise enough for first time visitors to this area. At 10:10 am, we arrived and parked in the lot at the end of the road near the boat dock and took the unmarked Meadowview Trail over to Hitching Post Loop Trail. Meadowview Trail merged with Hitching Post trail without a sign and a short distance later the path split. We kept to the right and followed this level easy trail to the junction of Walnut Creek. This is where we figured out, according to the handout, we were on Hitching Post Loop Trail. We walked Turkey Track trail crossing the quaint Walnut Creek and veered onto the narrow rocky path that followed the creek, aptly named Walnut Creek Trail.

At its end we came to a complete intersection of pathways which turned out to be the intersection of Walnut Creek, Turkey Track, and its connector path to a neighboring subdivision. The time was 11:30. We took a left and followed Turkey Track trail back up to Hitching Post Loop Trail and followed the rest of its loop trail to where it came out on the paved loop trail around the lake. It is here that we found its trailhead marker for Hitching Post Loop. Along the way we saw the sign for the Big Springs connector path, but it didn't say how far this path went before it connected up. We finished our total hike at 12:35. Over all we spent 2 ½ hours enjoying a beautiful May day in the park and spotted one elk.

NOTE: As of 2003 this area is in the process of being purchased by the city so that it can remain and not be developed.

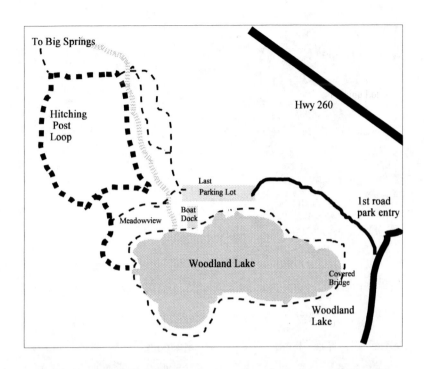

To Big Springs

Hitching
Post
Loop

Hwy 260

Last
Parking Lot

Boat
Dock

Meadowview

1st road
park entry

Woodland Lake

Covered
Bridge

Woodland
Lake

# OLD HATCHERY TRAIL (a.k.a. OLD HATCHERY BRIDGE TRAIL, PINETOP FISH HATCHERY TRAIL) (One way)

*"Those who know Your name will trust in You, for You, Lord, have never forsaken those who seek You" (Psalm 9:10).*

LOCATION: Pinetop

**The Walk**
LENGTH: ½ mile (one way)
RATE: Easy
TIME: 45 minutes (round trip)

ELEVATION: 7500'
USE: Infrequent
PARKING: Plenty

DIRECTIONS: Trailhead is in the parking lot of the AZ Fish & Game Department, 2878 West White Mountain Blvd in Pinetop. It is marked with the blue diamonds of the W.M.T.S. (although I haven't found a trail number assigned to it). Access to it is also through a gate found along Hwy 260 (100 yards +/- past Hill Drive). Hill Drive is the last street on the left before you get to the AZ Fish & Game Dept. In May of 1999, this land along the highway was up for sale, so it is unknown if this trail access point will remain. There is also a sign for it along the Springs Trail. If you are hiking the Springs Trail and have an extra hour to leisurely enjoy this one way side trip, it is well worth it.

WHO I WENT WITH, DATE, & MY NOTES

DESCRIPTION: I caught this trail off of the Springs Trail. It isn't mentioned in the W.M.T.S. booklet and as of 9/14/99, it didn't have a trail number. The trail sign called it the Old Hatchery Bridge Trail and that it was ½ a mile long. A lovely trail that wanders along the creek to the old fish hatchery area. Across the bridge and up the hill is where I came out to the highway near by the AZ Fish & Game Dept. Their phone number is 928) 367-4281.

70

HISTORY: The Hatchery Trail leads past an old fish hatchery that was built in the early 1930's. At that time, Pinetop was the major trout hatchery and rearing station in this state. Up to 3 million fish eggs a year were hatched here. In 1954, with the failure of steady water supply during a dry period, the hatchery was closed. You'll notice some of its concrete structures which are still standing.

The trail was constructed with a grant from the AZ Game and Fish Department's Heritage Fund and additional funding from the Town of Pinetop-Lakeside. TRACK volunteers built the bridge over Billy Creek and continued the trail to where it connects to the Springs Trail.

*No trail map needed. It is well marked.*

Author

# IRON HORSE "CONNECTOR" TRAIL
## #632a (COUNTRY CLUB TO SPRINGS)
## (One way)

*"The Lord detests all the proud of heart. Be sure of this: They will not go unpunished" (Proverbs 16:5).*

LOCATION: Pinetop

**The Walk**
LENGTH:  A bit over 2 miles (one way)
RATE:  Easy
TIME:  1 ½ hrs (round trip)

DIRECTIONS:  Follow the directions to the Country Club Trailhead on page 61.

USE: Infrequent
PARKING: Good

WHO I WENT WITH, DATE, & MY NOTES

TRAIL DIRECTION:  Follow Country Club trail on its single narrow dirt path through the woods for .64 of a mile.where it'll come to a cross road. Take a right at this junction and continue to follow the blue diamonds with the green dot. The sign reads 1.5 miles to the Springs Trailhead. The trail now follows a old logging road for a time and then narrows down again until you come out a forest gate on the road roughly opposite the Springs Trailhead.

ELEVATION:  7200'

# PINECREST "ACCESS" TO BLUE RIDGE TRAIL IN BILLY CREEK TRAILS PARK (One way)

*"And Jesus said My job down here on earth is to get sinners back to God - not to worry about the good people" (Matthew 9:13b).*

ATTRACTION: Riparian environment, multiple trails

LOCATION: Pinetop

**The Walk**
LENGTH: .89 (one way)
RATE: Easy
TIME: 30 minutes (one way)

DIRECTIONS: From Show Low (intersection of the Deuce & White Mtn. Rd.) head south on White Mtn. Rd. to Lakeside. A short distance pass the mini-

WHO I WENT WITH, DATE, & MY NOTES

shopping complex with its large grocery store & theater, you will be making a left turn on Pinecrest Avenue (at the Best Western Inn) and follow a short distance (0.2) to park at the road's dead end. There is a forest service "V" walk-through. Trailhead indicates the trail as being Blue Ridge Trail #107 which is half a mile ahead on foot.

USE: Moderate                    PARKING: Very limited
ELEVATION: 6,940 - 7,026 ft.

TRAIL DIRECTION: Start by following the blue diamond marked trail for Blue Ridge. Turn left at the "T" intersection. You'll continue to follow this portion of the Blue Ridge Access Trail. In less than a mile (.89) the path will come to the creek where you will feel led to follow. After crossing the creek, you'll be on the Blue Ridge Trail. Heading to the left leads to Blue Ridge Trailhead #1 or heading to the immediate right, along the creek, will lead you to Blue Ridge Trailhead #2 and the Little Bear 'connector' to Springs Trail.

CONNECTORS: The Blue Ridge Trail has a green dot attached to the blue diamond denoting it as an connector trail. It is considered as connecting with the Pinecrest Street over into Woodland Lake Park. However, because there are residential blocks and Hwy 260 dividing the two I am calling this an 'access' trail. Be aware that not all the necessary blue diamonds will have the green dots to properly indicate that the path you are following in Billy Creek Trails Park is the 'connector' to Blue Ridge Trail that you may be seeking.

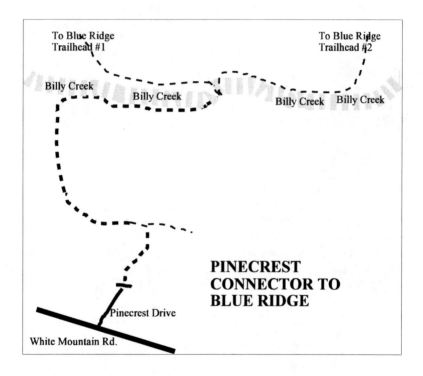

To Blue Ridge Trailhead #1

To Blue Ridge Trailhead #2

Billy Creek

Billy Creek

Billy Creek

Billy Creek

**PINECREST CONNECTOR TO BLUE RIDGE**

Pinecrest Drive

White Mountain Rd.

ALERT! Be on the look out for poison ivy plants growing close to the ground. They have three leaves and are bright green in color.

Until fairly recently, the widespread Poison Ivy was thought to be two distinct species: "Poison Ivy," a vine with pointed leaflets; and "Poison Oak," a shrubby plant with oak-like leaflets. But when cuttings from the same plant were grown in different locations, both forms were produced. Those in moist, shady forests became poison ivy vines; those in dry, sunny places grew into poison oak plants.

## No Trail Map is Completely Accurate
Billy Creek Trails Park consists of over 220 acres providing an excellent area for nature study or bird watching. A wide variety of flowers along the creek and in the canyon area can be seen. It is a popular area for walking due to its proximity to Lakeside and Pinetop and its several unmarked trails.

Our first trip to this trails park was an experience in not paying attention to signs. I had the Parks & Rec's map of the 'Billy Creek 2.7 Mile Loop' in hand and after verifying the four entry points marked on it, we drove to the Pinecrest Avenue entry and proceeded to hike what I thought was the Billy Creek Trail as outlined on the map I held. At this entry point the trail is marked with a blue diamond. The kiosk's maps weren't of use. There is a wood sign with arrow saying Blue Ridge ½ a mile ahead. However, we ignored this sign because we were determined to follow the map that I had and hike the 2.7 'Billy Creek Loop Trail'. After walking far more than the 2.7 miles, we had to admit we weren't on the right trail and had to retrace our footsteps because daylight was fading. What we had ended up doing was walking the Blue Ridge Connector all the way to the Little Bear Connector which leads to the Springs Trail. There weren't any trail numbered blue diamonds, which would have helped!

I don't give up easily and decided that come Memorial Day weekend I would head out again to verify the Billy Creek Loop Trail. Memorial Weekend sees this area swell up, tripling its normal population. I thought for sure I would encounter a lot of people, but I didn't encounter anyone! Entering the forest from Pineview Drive, I walked the short distance to where a wide dirt road intersects the narrow trail. Armed again with the faxed trail map from the Lakeside Park & Rec. Dept., I followed this path to the right. It is very wide and level. I followed it and saw where numerous other trails take off from it, hence giving its name "trails park." After a half hour trying to find the circuitous route outlined on the map, I realized that half of this trail no longer exists. Also, I couldn't find a single trail marker for Billy Creek Loop.

In June of 1999, I called the Pinetop-Lakeside Recreation Department and was informed that this trails park wasn't going to become an official park of the White Mountain Trail System (W.M.T.S.) because of the Goshawk. The Goshawk is a bird of prey that is being studied by the forest ranger station to determine if establishing this trail would endanger it. I asked a TRACKS member (June 1999) about it and she said its been part of the ranger's study for over five years. The handout map Pinetop-Lakeside gives out on Billy Creek Trails park is dated as being revised 4/91.

Later in June of 1999 I called and talked with the Lakeside Ranger Station about tree markings and the Goshawk. I was told that there is a nesting Goshawk by Billy Creek and the trails park will not be developed. Goshawks are like chicken hawks. They fly low and in between trees and part of their diets consist of squirrels and rabbits.

---

TIDBIT ~Tree markings consist of paint. Blue means "to cut", yellow "not cut", orange for marking boundary, and black paint used to correct mistakes. Blue ribbons signify boundaries. This type and color code may be specific only to our area.

# SHOW LOW

## Loop Trails
Buena Vista #637
Show Low City Park

## One Way Trails
Fool Hollow Lake Recreation Area
Show Low Lake
Summit Sidewalk

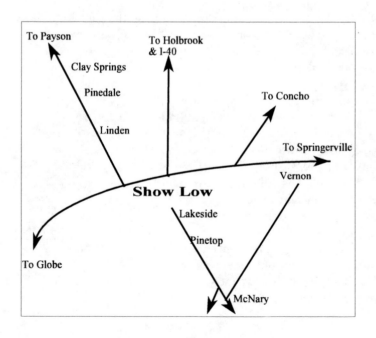

# BUENA VISTA TRAIL #637 (Loop)

*"I will praise God's name in song and glorify Him with thanksgiving"*
*(Psalm 69:30).*

ATTRACTION: Panoramic views

LOCATION: Show Low

**The Walk**
LENGTH: 9 miles                              RATE: Moderate
TIME: 5 hours

DIRECTIONS: From the corner of the gas station & Victorian Building (Hwys 60, 77, 260 intersection) head 2.8 miles on Hwy 77 in the direction of Globe. Turn left on FR 300 and the trailhead is on your immediate left.

USE: Moderate                              PARKING: Plenty
TRAVEL DIRECTION: Clockwise     ELEVATION: 6520' - 6773'

DESCRIPTION: In ten minutes (½ a mile) the path comes to a 'T' intersection where it becomes a loop trail. It is suggested to go clockwise in direction, so take a left here. The trail follows portions of old logging roads through pine, oak, and manzanita. Because of so many roads, be sure to keep your eyes open to follow the blue diamonds. In a quarter of a mile, you'll see a post with a blue diamond and arrow pointing to the right. From here it is only another fifth of a mile before you come to the 0.07 short cut which veers to your right. You'll find the terrain relatively hilly and there are hills you'll have to traverse, but at various points you will be able to see off for great distances. It is a great hike on a beautiful day. Keep your eye out for animal signs. You should be able to spot racoon prints and coyote scat.

WHO I WENT WITH, DATE, & MY NOTES

SHORT CUT(S) ~Taking a left at the 'T', continue in this clockwise direction and in about another half mile, you'll come to a blue diamond with two yellow dots to indicate the short cut. This shortcut path is only 0.7 long. It connects to the opposite side of the Buena Vista trail cutting off about 7 miles. At the end of this short cut, take a right and in a little over a mile (1.19) you'll come back to the 'T' intersection. Making a left here will take you back to the trailhead. All in all this is a 2.7 mile hike.

CONNECTOR TRAIL TO LOS CABALLOS "The Chihuahua Pine" is reached by following the Buena Vista trail clockwise for 2 miles. You can reach it by taking a left at the 'T' where Buena Vista becomes a loop trail. Keep your eyes open for the blue diamond with two plastic green dots. In following this connector trail, just keep veering to the right when it intersects with other dirt roads paths. It is well marked with diamonds. If in doubt, just veer to your right. This trail becomes a wide path, easily walked, and in less than a mile (0.88) you will come to the highway (mile post marker 338). This is where the trail goes down to a bright lavender painted underpass to the other side of Hwy 260 and continues its way to connecting to the Los Caballos Trail, about 4.5 miles further. This trail was completed by the TRACKS organization in the late summer of 1999 (see page 48).

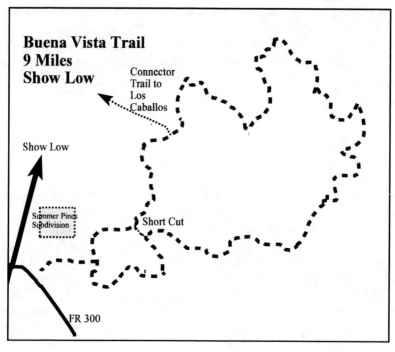

**Buena Vista Trail
9 Miles
Show Low**

Connector
Trail to
Los
Caballos

Show Low

Summer Pines
Subdivision

Short Cut

FR 300

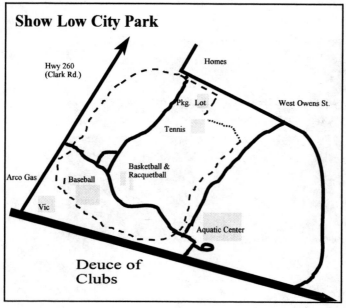

# Show Low City Park

Hwy 260
(Clark Rd.)

Homes

Pkg. Lot

West Owens St.

Tennis

Arco Gas

Basketball &
Racquetball

Baseball

Vic

Aquatic Center

**Deuce of
Clubs**

# SHOW LOW CITY PARK (Loop)

*"My steps have held to Your paths; my feet have not slipped" (Psalms 17:5).*

ATTRACTION: Paved, within city limits, easy access and wheel chair accessible. Interpretive signs along the path.

LOCATION: Show Low

**The Walk**

WHO I WENT WITH, DATE, & MY NOTES

LENGTH: 1.1 miles
RATE: Easy                    TIME: 25 minutes

DIRECTIONS: On the corner of the Victorian Building, gas station, and the Mormon church (Hwys 60, 260, 77). There are four entrances to the park.

USE: Heavy                              PARKING: Plenty
ELEVATION: 6300'

DESCRIPTION: A paved loop that takes you around the perimeter of the entire park. The park boasts outdoor baseball fields, tennis courts, indoor (very poor condition) racquetball courts, basketball courts, children's play areas, volleyball courts, and pavilions. On one corner sits the large public indoor swimming pool facility.

In addition to the interpretive signs the trail has physical workout stations along it for fitness training. The trail is marked with blue diamonds, but does not have a number assigned to it because it isn't on forest service property. It is hard to believe, but apparently no published information exists on this paved loop. I've asked. The real nice feature of this trail is that you can start and end wherever you feel like.

*Trail map located on previous page.*

# FOOL HOLLOW LAKE RECREATION AREA (One way)

*"And even now the axe of God's judgment is poised to chop down every unproductive tree. They will be chopped and burned"*
*(Matthew 3:10).*

ATTRACTION: Lake view

LOCATION: Show Low

COST: As of 1999 the park's entrance fee for day use is $5.00.

**The Walk**
LENGTH: 2 miles (round trip)
RATE: Easy
TIME: 1 hour (round trip)

WHO I WENT WITH, DATE, & MY NOTES

GATE: The entrance gate is open during the day and closed during the night between 10:00 pm and 5:00 am. The park is open year round.

DIRECTIONS: From the Show Low Post Office head west and turn right on Hwy 260 towards Heber/Overgaard. Follow the highway (a.k.a. Clark Road) 2 miles to Old Linden Road, making a right turn and going to the park entrance on your left. Follow to park entrance. Pick up a map at the entrance booth. Past the entrance booth, you take a right at the first intersection and follow the long road down to the "T" cross road and turn left. Follow this road to its end at the boat dock. Park and walk down to the dock on the left side of the parking lot. There is no trailhead, but the trail starts off near the edge of the boat dock and lake.

USE: Moderate                           PARKING: Plenty
ELEVATION: 6,300 ft.

DESCRIPTION: An 800-acre recreation area offering playgrounds, picnicking, camping, boating, fishing, birding, and wildlife viewing. The 150 acre lake was finished in 1994 through a partnership between AZ

State Parks, US Forest Service, AZ Game & Fish, City of Show Low and corporate sponsors AZ Public Service and McCarthy Construction Company.

HISTORY: The tiny town of Adair has long since been covered over by the lake, but it was Aaron Adair who was responsible for the name Fool Hollow. In 1885, Adair moved into the area with the intention of farming. The locals joked that only a fool would try and farm the place. The name stuck! Show Low Creek flows into Fool Hollow Lake, providing a natural feeding ground for a variety of wildlife and many kinds of fish

DESCRIPTION: An easy one way and level trail taking you around the southern half of the lake. My friend, Gracie Kelley, and I enjoyed a beautiful September day to casually walk this trail which is a real gem within the City of Show Low; albeit you have to pay $5.00 to gain entrance into this park. I noticed plenty of places to sit and a few individuals taking advantage of rocks and downed trees to do just this. There are pavilions on the west side to enjoy having a meal. All in all it took us one and half hours to walk the entire trail because we walked slow and did a lot of talking.

As you walk near the lake you'll notice wire cages around the base of some trees. This is to prevent resident beavers from dining on them. The beaver's powerful jaws and sharp teeth enable it to cut a 5 inch tree in under five minutes and occasionally fall trees up to two feet in diameter. To construct a dam, they poke felled logs into the stream bed, then pile sticks, mud and gravel around making it almost impregnable. The lodge itself starts out as a solid mound of sticks and mud, then rooms and various escape tunnels are gnawed out for the inside.

Although beavers are nocturnal, they can sometimes be spotted during the day. Beaver, which weight up to 60 lbs are the largest rodents in North America and one extremely well-suited for their aquatic life. They are excellent swimmers using their broad flat tail and partially webbed hind feet for propulsion. They can stay underwater for up to 15 minutes and are equipped with special transparent membranes which cover their eyes, allowing them to see well under the water. They even have an oil gland which allows them to waterproof their heavy fur coat.

Unfortunately I have never spotted a beaver or their tell tale signs at Fool Hollow Lake and only have the word of a park ranger to account for their existence in the park.

Besides being on the lookout for beaver sign, keep your eyes scanning the sky for circling birds of prey like the distinctive bald eagle or white Osprey. The Osprey, sometimes called a "fish hawk" is indeed a skillful fisherman, plunging feet first into the water to retrieve its prey. But, few can match the airborne hunting ability of the eagle's keen eyesight. With great skill the bald eagle will fold its wings and sweep quickly down for the kill. Eagles have also been known to bully Ospreys into dropping their catch, then nab it in mid-air.

*You'll be given a copy of the Fool Hollow Lake Recreation Area Site Map at the state park's entry station.*

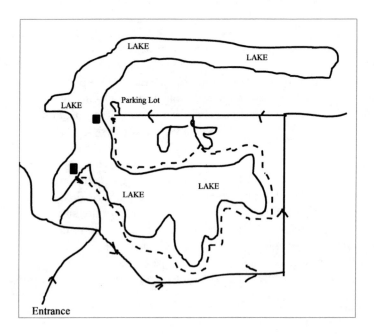

# SHOW LOW LAKE TRAIL(One way)

*"Then the angel of the LORD stood in a narrow path between two vineyards, with walls on both sides" (Numbers 22:24).*

ATTRACTION: Lake view

LOCATION: Show Low

**The Walk**
RATE: Easy
TIME: 15 minutes (one way)

DIRECTIONS: From the Deuce of Clubs, take White Mountain Road south towards Lakeside. Turn left at the signal light intersection of Navapache Hospital & WalMart Supercenter. Follow Show Low Lake Road one mile to the lake's damn. Look for an entrance on the left side that looks like it goes straight into a campground. Drive to the right past the campground and follow the road the short distance to its end. Park and walk past the green rail and you will see the narrow dirt trail.

WHO I WENT WITH, DATE, & MY NOTES

USE: Very little                              PARKING: Plenty
ELEVATION: 6500'

DESCRIPTION: A narrow and rocky path that follows along the north side of the lake. It is best to go in very dry conditions. The path pretty much ends at a gate. Past the gate the trail continues a short bit up to electric power poles where it disappears for good.

COMMENTS: This trail appears to be no longer maintained. The nearby camp store has no information on it. You may find it mentioned, like I did, in an undated and outdated handout from the forest ranger station in Lakeside.

*This trail is not maintained. No trail map available.*

# SUMMIT TRAIL (SIDEWALK) (One way)

*"For whosoever shall call upon the name of the Lord shall be saved"*
*(Romans 10:13).*

ATTRACTION: Wheel-chair accessible
LOCATION: Show Low

**The Walk**
LENGTH: 1.9 miles (one way)
RATE: Easy & Wheelchair accessible.
TIME: 40 minutes (one way)

WHO I WENT WITH, DATE, &
MY NOTES

DIRECTIONS: From Show Low's west-end intersection of the gas station & Victorian Building, head a very shor t one eighth (.8) of a mile in the direction of Globe. You'll notice the green Summit Trail sign. Turn right into the Torreon subdivision entrance. Parking is on your immediate right. You'll see the sidewalk.

USE: Infrequent                                            PARKING: Limited
ELEVATION: 6300'

TRAVEL DIRECTION: From the Visitor's Center side off of Hwy. 77. See directions above.

DESCRIPTION: By the time this book is published, this sidewalk will have been dedicated to the public. The sidewalk skirts along the golf course and through the Torreon subdivision ending at Clark Road (a.k.a. Hwy. 260).

COMMENT: Although this isn't what is defined as a 'trail', it does make for a lovely walk, and it is wheel-chair accessible.

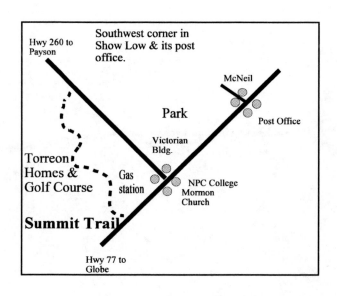

Hwy 260 to
Payson

Southwest corner in
Show Low & its post
office.

McNeil

Park

Post Office

Victorian
Bldg.

Torreon
Homes &
Golf Course

Gas
station

NPC College
Mormon
Church

Summit Trail

Hwy 77 to
Globe

Bellflower

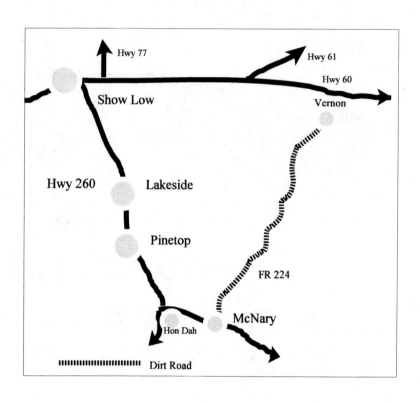

# VERNON

## Loop Trails
Land of the Pioneers #629
Los Burros #631

## Connector Trails
Chipmunk Springs #631a
  (Los Burros / Country Club)
Four Springs #629a
  (Los Burros / Land of the Pioneers)

## Access Trails
Four Springs at Lake Mountain

# LAND OF THE PIONEERS TRAIL #629
## (Loop)

*"God is spirit and His worshipers must worship in spirit
and in truth" (John 4:24).*

LOCATION: Vernon

**The Walk**
LENGTH: 11 miles
RATE: Moderate
TIME: 7 hours

WHO I WENT WITH, DATE, & MY NOTES

DIRECTIONS: From Show Low's post office head 19.5 miles east on Hwy 60. You won't see any signs saying 'Vernon' until you get to the gas station which marks the road in to Vernon. Take a right which is FR 224 and follow it through the Vernon for 5.3 miles, making a right on FR 5. You'll spot the trailhead on your right 0.6 miles ahead.

DIRECTION TRAVELED: Counter-clockwise
PARKING: Limited
ELEVATION RANGE: 7220' - 7866'
MOUNTAIN(S): Eckes

USE: Little

SHORT LOOP: A shortcut is marked bypassing Eckes Mountain, cutting off about one third of the overall trail distance. A new shortcut created in the summer of 1999, and numbered as 629b is ½ mile long. The short loop is seven miles long.

SPUR: Vista Point Trail lies at the base of Ecks Mountain and will take you to the top yielding a weeping view to the east and of Green's Peak. According to my pedometer it was 6.25 miles to the Ecks Mtn. Spur sign and walking up to this vista view was 1/3 a mile, not the .25 mile as posted. Also, it is a steep grade, making it a treacherous walk because of loose rock. Be extra careful on your way down.

CONNECTOR TRAIL(S): To Los Burros and Lake Mountain Spur (a.k.a Four Springs Access). The connector trails are located at the end of the short loop trail nearest Ecks Mtn.

HISTORY: The trail got its name from the several homesteads established in the area. There is a legend of three "Arab" women who were rumored to be rich and having stashed their money on their property. Someone believed the rumor and murdered them and torn their homestead apart to no avail. The foundations and parts of structures still remain, as do the lilac bushes they planted. You'll see these along the way at the 1.89 mile (45 minutes).

The old stones and logs represent a simpler life in the past, filled with hardships of the people who settled in this wilderness, who are aptly named pioneers.

In the year 2000, this trail was designated as a Millennium Trail by the White House Millennium Council. This special designation was through the efforts of the TRACKS volunteer organization, along with the Lakeside Ranger District. It is recognized as a trail that *"brings the community together to honor the past and imagine the future"* by connecting people to their land, history, and culture.

The trail is heavily wooded yet provides a few spectacular panoramic views. Most of the southern portion of this trail is made up of logging roads that, because of lack of tree cover can get pretty hot. Bring plenty of water. Logging roads are not shown on following map.

AUTHOR'S NOTE: We backpacked this trail in May 2000. I used the W.M.T.S. guidebook to follow the trail along with the guidance of the blue diamonds nailed to the trees. There were two points where we missed the trial largely due to the logging roads that repeatedly and randomly make up this trail. Upon finishing the trail, I noticed that both the kiosk map and the W.M.T.S. guidebook were wrong. Going clockwise on this trail you loop back without ever joining the beginning part of the trail as shown.

I clocked over 13 miles on my pedometer walking this trail. Don't forget, to add in perhaps 1 extra hour to allow for mistakes. This trail is a bit on the hard side to follow. Should you decide to make a two day journey of this trail, see *Backpacker's List of What to Take* on page 21 in the Reference List section of this book.

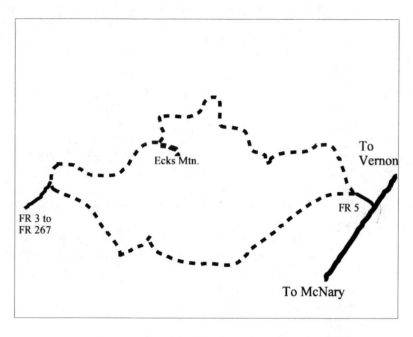

*Connectors & short cuts are not shown in above map.*

# LOS BURROS TRAIL #631 (Loop)

*"Don't lie, speak the truth with all others, for we are all one big family"*
*(Ephesians 4:25).*

ATTRACTION: Abundance of wildlife

LOCATION: Vernon / Pinetop (halfway between McNary & Vernon). The Los Burros Trail starts at the Los Burros campground.

**The Walk**
DISTANCE: 13 miles
TIME: 6 hours
RATE: Moderate
ELEVATION RANGE: 7825' - 8370'
DIRECTION TRAVELED: Counter-clockwise

DIRECTIONS: From Show Low head through Pinetop to McNary. In the middle of town look for the small sign saying 'Vernon' (FR 224). Turn left (north) and follow this dirt road for 7.1 miles. Turn right into Los Burros Campground and the trailhead is at the far end. The Fort Apache Indian Reservation borders the southern portion of this trail. Forest Roads 9 and 26 intersect trail.

WHO I WENT WITH, DATE, & MY NOTES

PARKING: Plenty                                    USE: Little
NAMES OF MOUNTAIN(S): Wishbone, Pierce & Lake Mountain

HISTORY: The Los Burros Ranger Station used to be at the campground, evident by two of the original buildings still existing. The trail passes through heavy forest and offers plenty of opportunity to spot wildlife.

SHORT LOOP(S): A new short cut was under construction in the summer of 1999. It will be assigned the number 631b.

93

CONNECTOR TRAIL(S): The connector "Chipmunk Springs" heads west to the Country Club Trail in Pinetop. The other one is "Four Springs" which leads to Land of the Pioneers Trail.

CAMPGROUND: Camping is free. There is usually a camp host in the summer. Tables, barbecue pits, and outhouses are on site, however no water or trash cans were noticed.

SPUR TRAIL: There is a spur trail to the top of Lake Mountain taking you to the lookout tower there. This spur trail is located along the path when you get near Lake Mountain. It is a steep climb upward approximately 1.25 miles. I rate it hard.

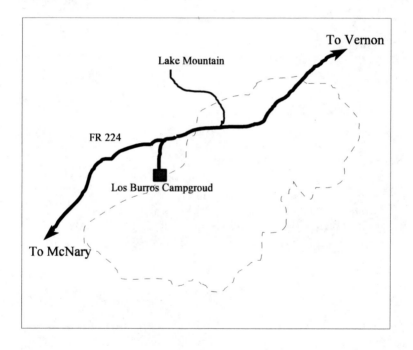

*Connector trails are not shown on above map.*

## Los Burros Trail #631

In July of 2000, my husband (Al), dogs, and I drove to Los Burros campground with the day plans to use the shortcut to hike the southern portion of Los Burros. It was a lovely 8 miles and an easy hike. Beautiful with the meadows and aspen groves. A well-marked trail. No doubt as to where to go at any time. It was a picture perfect day, and we couldn't have had a better time. From the campground's trailhead you walk a quarter of a mile to a "T" intersection where you can go left, straight, or right. We went right because I wanted to do this trail counter-clockwise. As it turns out this was the best way to go given the fact it was more down hill in nature than uphill. After we turned right it was 3/5ths of a mile until we came to FR 8. Shortly after crossing this road, we took a twenty minute break to rest the dogs. It was a total of 5.8 miles to the short cut back to the trailhead. The short cut is 1 ½ miles long. The total loop we took that day was 8.06 miles and we finished in 4 hours with a total of 35 minutes in two rest breaks. We never saw anyone on this trail, but did see four elk.

A couple of weeks later we went camping in Los Burros with plans of hiking the other half of this trail plus, we decided to backtrack to the Four Spring 'spur' trail to see if the signs made sense going to the nearby spur, access, and connector trails relating to Four Springs and Land of the Pioneers trail from this point. We traveled clockwise. I suggest traveling counter-clockwise. Going clockwise from the trailhead you'll face going uphill for the bulk of trail. It's easier going counter-clockwise.

We clocked 9.96 miles on the brand new pedometer for that day. We went from the campground out to the "T" (.025) and went left. 1.69 miles later we crossed McNary road and 1.5 miles later we crossed McNary road again and started the climb around Wishbone Mountain. Pierce Springs (and tank) had foul drinking water, which our dogs drank and later on became sick. The trail is well marked and several miles later we came to the short cut (1.5 miles) trail and from there it was an easy shot home (campground).

This trail is diversified in the terrain you travel through. There is a good stretch of woods that shows new growth and history of fire. There are areas with thick ferns and groves of Aspen trees.

For a leisurely, albeit long, hike, don't forget to go counter-clockwise. *P.S. The dogs did get well by the next day.*

# CHIPMUNK SPRINGS "CONNECTOR" TRAIL #631a (LOS BURROS TO COUNTRY CLUB) (One way)

*"He himself bore our sins in His body on the tree, so that we might die to sins and live for righteousness; by His wounds you have been healed" (1 Peter 2:24).*

LOCATION: Vernon / Pinetop

**The Walk**

DISTANCE: 6.5 - 7 miles　　　　　　　　TIME: 4 hours

RATE: Moderate　　　　ELEVATION RANGE: 7200' - 7800'

DIRECTIONS: From McNary: From Show Low head through Pinetop to McNary and turn left on FR 224 (marked 'to Vernon') and follow this dirt road for 7.1 miles. Turn right into the Los Burros Campground and the trailhead is at the far end (page 93). From Pinetop: From Show Low head to Pinetop turning left on Bucksprings Road, drive ½ a mile and turn left again on Sky High Road (FR 182). Country Club Trailhead (page 61) is two miles ahead on the right.

WHO I WENT WITH, DATE, & MY NOTES

PARKING: Plenty　　　　USE: Very little

MOUNTAIN(S): Brushy

*Trail map on next page.*

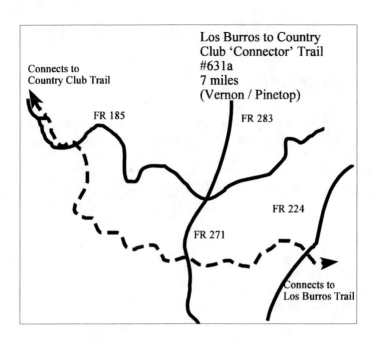

Los Burros to Country Club 'Connector' Trail #631a 7 miles (Vernon / Pinetop)

Connects to Country Club Trail

FR 185

FR 283

FR 224

FR 271

Connects to Los Burros Trail

Thistle

# FOUR SPRINGS "CONNECTOR" TRAIL
## #629a (LOS BURROS TO LAND OF THE PIONEERS) (One way)

*"The fear of the Lord is the beginning of knowledge, but fools despise wisdom and discipline" (Proverbs 1:7).*

ATTRACTION: Springs

LOCATION: McNary area to Vernon

**The Walk**
LENGTH: 8 miles
RATE: Moderate
TIME: 4 hrs, plus time to get to and from the trailheads

DIRECTIONS: From Show Low head through Pinetop to McNary and turn left on FR 224 (marked 'to Vernon') and follow this dirt road for 7.1 miles. Turn right into the Los Burros Campground and the trailhead is at the far end. Walk this trail to the 'T' intersection and follow it to the left. You'll cross over McNary Road (another starting point) and follow it to the connector sign that reads Four Springs 629a. This is the trail you want.

WHO I WENT WITH, DATE, & MY NOTES

From Land of the Pioneers Trail (page 90): The connector trail is approximately 6.25 miles from the trailhead traveling counter-clockwise. It is located near Ecks Mtn.

USE: Infrequent                    PARKING: Plenty

DESCRIPTION: This connector trail traverses for 8 miles between Eden, Brown, Dipping Vat, and Mudd springs (hence the trail name). Dipping Vat Spring, the site of a historic sheep camp, still displays some remnants of a dipping vat several hundred feet to the north of the tank.

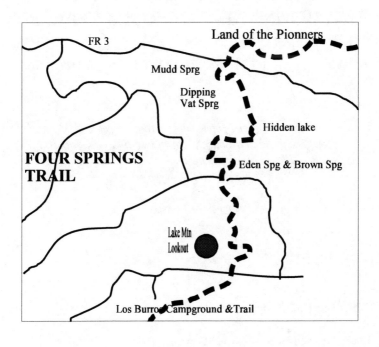

# FOUR SPRINGS "ACCESS" TRAIL
## LAKE MOUNTAIN LOOKOUT TOWER TO FOUR SPRINGS CONNECTOR TRAIL #629A (a.k.a. FOUR SPRINGS 'SPUR' TRAIL (One way)

*"Listen! I hear the voice of someone shouting 'Make a road for the Lord through the wilderness; make Him a straight, smooth road through the desert. Fill the valley; level the hills; straighten out the crooked paths and smooth off the rough spots in the road'" (Isaiah 40:3,4).*

LOCATION: Between Vernon & McNary

**The Walk**
LENGTH: .50
RATE: Easy on way down, moderate on the way back up.
TIME: 1 hr round trip

DIRECTIONS: From Show Low head through Pinetop to McNary. Look for the small green sign marked 'Vernon" and turn left (FR 224) and follow this dirt road for 9 miles to road #267 and turn left. Stay on this road .2 miles, then left on Rd. 269. Follow this road up to the top, parking

WHO I WENT WITH, DATE, & MY NOTES

near the trailhead just below the lookout tower. Walking the path approximately 3/4ths of a mile you will come to the (8.5 mile) connector trail on your left which leads to the Land of the Pioneers trail. (Just a reminder, any connector trail you decide to hike, you should also consider that you'll come out at some point during your destination trail and will still have to follow that trail perhaps miles to get to *its* trailhead.) At this point if you continue straight on the path you'll get to a 'T' intersection. To the left and right is the Los Burros trail. Going to the right is the shortest route to Los Burros Campground.

DESCRIPTION: The 4 Springs Trail is a access trail *leading to* the connector trail for Los Burros #631 and Land of the Pioneers #629. Its trailhead is just below Lake Mountain Look Out Tower.

DEDICATION: The access trail "Lake Mountain Lake" is dedicated to the memory of Kathy Ibsen, who was killed in 1998 from an auto accident in Salt River Canyon. It isn't posted as to how long the access trail is. I walked down a short distance to the lake (which was nothing, but grass in August) and found such a diversified abundance of mushrooms, that I never did go any further in walking. (Be sure to see my section on mushrooms later on in this book.)

HIGHLIGHTS: After a particular heavy summer monsoon season, one might find an abundance of mushrooms. In August of 1999, I found at least 10 different kind, generating my interest and a special mention of them in this book. The trail itself circles the lake on top of the mountain. Lake Mountain is an old volcano and the lake fills in the depression during heavy rain/snow seasons.

## A Lesson Learned

In July 2000, after my husband, our three dogs, and I hiked the 8 mile shortcut Los Burros loop, we headed up to Lake Mountain Lookout Tower with the intent of hiking this spur trail. We were into the hike about ½ a mile when I decided to go back to the truck, because it was going to rain and I had mistakenly left my backpack and its essential items behind. Al said he'd continue on and would join me at a rendezvous point if I would drive the truck down to McNary road where the Los Burros trail intersected it. He'd see me in less than an hour and he didn't mind if it rained. He kept our cocker spaniel, Pepsi, with him. I took the other two dogs, with me and went back to the truck and drove to the agreed upon location. And there I waited . . . and waited.

After 2 ½ hours I became concerned as daylight was fleeing, so I hiked the trail up to where I thought I had said goodbye to Al. The trail goes across the road leading to the lookout tower and then to two signs. One sign read Land of the Pioneers trail (green dot) and the other said Lake Mountain Spur trail (red dot), which is what I wanted. There was no sign of Al or the dog. I had to turn back because the daylight was almost gone. Back at the truck I saw darkness come with minimum amount of star light. It never did rain. Thank heavens, it had only sprinkled. The only thing that could possibly have happened was that somehow Al had gotten on the 4 Springs connector trail which led many miles away to intersect with Vernon's Land of the Pioneers trail. Surely after a few miles he'd realize he was on the wrong trail; going the wrong way? Why he didn't realize his mistake early on, is still a mystery, but sure enough, many miles, later, he came out where the trail intersects Land of the Pioneers. He didn't have enough daylight to walk the 7 miles back, so he forged on because he needed to find McNary road so he could walk it back to find me. He had another 4 miles to go before he reached that trailhead and then another half mile to just get to McNary Road. From there he knew he'd have 7 plus miles to walk on the road back to me.

Meanwhile back at the truck, I started praying, asking God to keep Al and Pepsi safe and returned. I prayed that God would provide them a ride back to me. God answered my prayers! It was night and very dark. I started driving determined to drive back and forth between Los Burros campground and Vernon until I found them. I didn't have to drive far before a white truck drove up to a stop beside me and there they were in the back of the pickup. Praise the Lord! I vowed once again, to keep the scripture throughout this book, because God has answered every prayer through our hikes and its subsequent writing. We didn't get the truck driver's name, but we thank that kind stranger who picked Al and the dog up just about a quarter of a mile down on McNary road. I am also glad that Al is in very good physical shape and that he did have extra water with him. To Pepsi it was a long adventure!

I asked Al how he could have gone wrong. He said that after I left he followed the mountain trail down another couple of switchbacks when he came to two arrows. One had a green dot, the other a red dot. He remembered me telling him green dots indicated connector trails and red dots were vista views. So he followed the green dotted blue diamonds thinking this was the connector to Los Burros. Not believing much in maps and with an ego that says "I know everything there is to know" he had a most humbling experience and acknowledges that the Good Lord provided the strength he needed and then the truck to carry him the rest of the way. He also saw a bear just off the trail, and Pepsi stayed by his side without veering away at any time during the journey.

Others could make a similar mistake. There shouldn't be a trailhead at the top of Lake Mountain and, in particular, one without a posted map. This is really a 'vista' view trail (red dots on blue diamonds) that should only be called out from the bottom of the mountain when a hiker is walking along the Four Springs Connector Trail and not from the top.

# NATURE STUDIES

Big Springs Environmental Study Area
Jacques Marsh
Pintail Lake (Alan Severson Habitat)

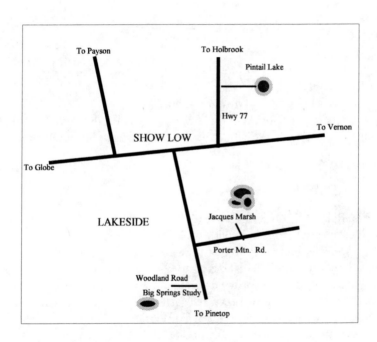

# BIG SPRINGS ENVIRONMENTAL STUDY AREA TRAIL *(NATURE STUDY)* #610 (Loop)

*"The Father loves the Son and has placed everything in His hands. Whosoever believes in the Son has eternal life, but whoever rejects the Son will not see life, for God's wrath remains on him" (John 4:36).*

ATTRACTION: Self-guided, riparian and birdwatching.

LOCATION: Lakeside

**The Walk**
DISTANCE: ½ mile
TIME: 20 minutes
RATE: Easy

WHO I WENT WITH, DATE, & MY NOTES

DIRECTIONS: From Show Low drive south on Highway 260 towards Pinetop. Turn right at the signal light on Woodland Road and continue about .6 miles. Parking lot and trailhead are on the left. Enter the area on foot.

PARKING: Plenty                    ELEVATION: 6,900 ft.
USE: Moderate

DESCRIPTION: Interpretative trail. Path follows along a riparian area. This is an easy ½ mile loop with streams, pond, benches and trail signs. Big Springs is a major source of pure crystal clear spring water flowing into Rainbow Lake. The lake is a storage reservoir for the Show Low Irrigation Company. It provides irrigation water for ranches and farms on the west side of Show Low Creek as well as farms and ranches in the Show Low valley area and beyond. The existence of fresh water shrimp in the waters immediately surrounding the spring as it bubbles forth from the ground is an indication of the purity of the water. It has never been known to go dry.

HISTORY: Big Springs Environmental Study Area was developed by the nearby Blue Ridge School District, Forest Service and the town of

Pinetop/Lakeside. It exists to educate people on the environment and to encourage appreciation and awareness about our natural surroundings. Numerous springs make up the wetlands. This habitat area provides year-round homes for many varieties of waterfowl. Information is provided along the trail describing the natural history, plants and wildlife in this area. Several benches are also provided. The 583 acre naturally wooded area is part of the Apache-Sitgreaves National Forest located within the town.

The Town of Pinetop-Lakeside manages 73 acres (Woodland Park) on a special use permit from the Lakeside Ranger District. Blue Ridge School District operates the 40 acre portion that comprises Big Springs Environmental Area on another special use permit. The 470 remaining acres between the two are managed by the Forest Service.

Big Springs is within walking distance of the Blue Ridge school campus, and is used as an "outdoor classroom" by the schools, as well as a nature study area for visitors and the community.

Visitors to the White Mountains can learn about the flora and fauna first hand by walking the one-half mile self-guided loop trail around the springs. It is an ideal place to get acquainted with the mountains before taking longer hikes. The trail meanders through several different kinds of wildlife habitat. Interpretive signs along the trail point out facts about snags (dead trees that are home for cavity nest birds,) springs, wetlands, meadows and streams.

Mammals that may be seen in the park include Abert's squirrel, elk, mule deer, raccoon, skunk, black bear, coyote, mule deer, muskrat, gray fox and Big Brown Bat.

Dozens of species of birds fly in and around the area, so it is a favorite haunt of bird watchers. Migratory waterfowl may be sighted in the spring and fall, and many stay all winter, including resident blue herons. Wintering bald eagles are also sighted frequently. Near the springs you'll find wild iris, cattail, watercress and willow. On the drier slopes are prickly pear cactus, narrow-leaf yucca, and native grasses.

Interpretive wildlife programs are offered in the summer months at a small amphitheater near the springs. Brochures are available at the Lakeside Ranger Station.

CONNECTOR TRAIL(S): Very short pathway to Hitching Post Loop Trail - 5 minutes tops! It's even marked with a blue diamond.

*No trail map necessary.*

Big Springs Entry Sign

# JACQUES MARSH WILDLIFE AREA

*"If your eye is pure, there'll be sunshine in your soul"*
*(Matthew 6:22).*

ATTRACTION:  Nature Study

LOCATION:  Lakeside

DIRECTIONS:  From Lakeside, just east of the
USFS Ranger Station, take Porter Mountain Road
for 1.5 miles to Juniper Drive. Turn left and
continue for .6 miles to the dirt parking area. The
latter half of Juniper Drive is a poorly maintained
dirt road. Drive slowly.

WHO I WENT WITH, DATE, &
MY NOTES

VIEWING NOTES:  The fenced area has no facilities. From the
parking area go through the gate and walk the berms. Berms are the
man-made raised dirt collars surrounding the habitat.

DESCRIPTION:  Jacques Marsh is a real treat for bird and wildlife
lovers. Common visitors are ducks, geese, shorebirds, rabbits, coyote,
fox, bobcat, elk and non-game birds, to name a few. It consists of more
than 120 acres of National Forest land. Pond areas total 96 acres
containing 7 ponds and 18 islands. The goal is to maintain and improve
waterfowl nesting, feeding, and resting habitat using available treated
effluent; and to provide hunting and educational use by the public.

HISTORY:  To solve pollution problems in local streams and lakes from
sewage overflow in the nearby area. Construction began in 1978 and was
completed in 1979. Effluent was introduced by 1981. Funding for the
marsh structures was provided by the Pinetop-Lakeside Sanitary District
and Apache-Sitgreaves National Forest, who also supplied the land.

Size: 120 acres

*No trail map necessary.*

# PINTAIL LAKE WETLANDS TRAIL #617 & ALAN SEVERSON HABITAT (*NATURE STUDY*) (a.k.a. PINTAIL LAKE WATERFOWL ENHANCEMENT AREA) (One way)

*"The heavens declare the glory of God; the skies proclaim the work of His hands"*
*(Psalm 19:1).*

ATTRACTION:  Bird watching

LOCATION:  Show Low

**The Walk**

DISTANCE:  One tenth of a mile to either the observation blind or the observation deck.

TIME:  5 minutes (one way)
RATE:  Easy

DIRECTIONS:  From the Show Low Post Office head east on the Deuce of Clubs and make a left on Hwy 77 north towards Snowflake/Taylor. Follow Hwy 77 north approximately 3.3 miles. Brown highway sign says "Pintail Lake." Turn right. Follow maintained dirt road to end. Park your car and follow the established trail about 300 yards to either the raised observation deck or observation blind. The trail to the blind is paved, the other graveled.

WHO I WENT WITH, DATE, & MY NOTES

USE:  Moderate

ELEVATION:  6,400 ft.

DESCRIPTION:  Pintail Lake offers a self-guided tour and serves as an excellent observation and study area for anyone interested in waterfowl and its habitat. Depending on the time of year, several wildlife species can be seen. Some waterfowl species you may see are:  Mallard, Northern Pintail, Cinnamon and Green-winged Teal, Northern Shoveler, and Gadwall. In addition, the marsh area attracts a variety of other wildlife including deer, elk, antelope, Bald Eagles, songbirds, numerous shorebirds and wading birds. Canadian Geese and other migratory birds often use the lake as a stopover and rest area during migration.

HISTORY: Established through the cooperation of Apache-Sitgreaves National Forest, AZ Game and Fish Dept., Show Low Sanitary District, and the City of Show Low in 1976. Actual construction began in 1977. Pintail Lake is on 47 acres and is the first of its kind in the Southwestern Region of the USDA Forest Service. Waterfowl habitat in North America is decreasing at the alarming rate of 2,000 acres per day, every day of the year. This habitat increases waterfowl and provides wastewater disposal. Marsh ecosystems have the ability to further treat wastewater by removing large quantities of organic nutrients. This process results in the lush growth of vegetation in the marsh systems.

Pintail Lake is dedicated to the memory of Al Severson, AZ Game and Fish Wildlife Manager who died in a helicopter crash in 1980.

*No trail map necessary.*

# LOOK OUT TOWERS

Juniper Ridge
Lake Mountain
Springer Mountain

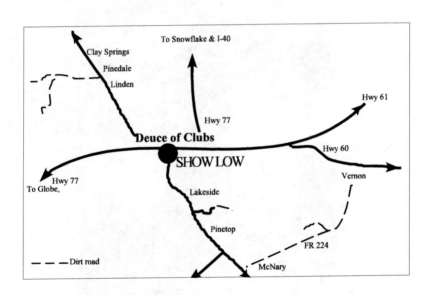

# JUNIPER RIDGE LOOKOUT (LINDEN)

ELEVATION: 6,998'
Hours posted

OPEN : Seasonal
Picnic area

DIRECTIONS: From Show Low head west on Hwy 260 (towards Payson). Keep an eye out for the sign Farnsworth Ranch Road (Old Highway 160) and turn left. Follow it to Juniper Ridge Lane (1.5 miles), turning left, and following this dirt road about 4 miles. Albeit it will feel like 20! The Juniper Ridge Trail cuts through here as well as criscrossing the road at one other point.

Juniper Ridge Lookout Tower

# LAKE MOUNTAIN LOOKOUT
## (VERNON-MCNARY)

OPEN: 8:00 - 4:30 during fire season.

DIRECTIONS: From Show Low head through Pinetop to McNary and turn left on FR 224 (marked 'to Vernon') and follow this dirt road for 9 miles to road #267 and turn left. Stay on this road .2 miles, then left on Rd. 269. Follow this road up to the top, parking near the trailhead just below the look out tower. The access trail to Four Springs Connector #629a is located here.

USE: light                    ELEVATION: 7,500 to 8,500 feet

This look out tower is on top of Lake Mountain. It was built in 1932. The Ponderosa Pine Tree you'll notice across from it was originally used as the lookout between 1912 and 1932. The tower is still used today and is opened to the public during the months of June and July. Its said that a beautiful scenic vista of the San Francisco Peaks can be seen on a clear day from the tower.

# SPRINGER MOUNTAIN LOOKOUT
## (LAKESIDE)

OPEN: 8:00 - 4:30 during fire season (end of May to Sept. depending on rains).

DIRECTIONS: Head to Pinetop. Turn left on Moonridge Drive (corner of Baptist Church and Pet Clinic) and follow to its end, turning right on Billy Creek Road, then a sharp left on Meadow Bridge. You'll drive across the creek and go right on Pine Shadow following its natural curve to the top of the hill looking for the imminent FR 187 on your right. Follow this poorly maintained dirt road 0.6 to the Look Out Tower sign. Turn right and proceed cautiously another half a mile. The Blue Ridge Trail #107 is nearby.

# WILDLIFE COMMUNITIES

# WILDLIFE

The enjoyment of wildlife is the primary focus of peoples' most popular outdoor recreational activity according to a survey by the U.S. Fish & Wildlife Service. Chipmunks and squirrels please us with their funny actions and deer with their benign graceful nature and soulful eyes. Although North America is home to some 400 species of mammals, most are by no means easy to find. The vast majority survive by being elusive.

Our rich wildlife of the Mogollon Rim country offers many opportunities for observing wild animals, from common campground birds like Steller's Jay to the majestic bull elk.

The keys to successful viewing are silence, stillness, patience, and a knowledge of the animal's habits. Dawn and dusk are the best times.

Generally, birds are the most commonly observed wildlife. Mammals are secretive by nature and, aside from squirrels and chipmunks, sightings are not common. Binoculars can be of great help. Tracks in muddy areas or in snow will tell about the wildlife that's been around if you know how to read the signs. I've included a section on identifying animal prints.

Much of the excitement of wildlife viewing stems from the fact that you can never be sure what you may see. Although some days are better than others, there are several things you can do to greatly increase your odds of seeing wildlife:

* Visit in the early morning and late evening.
* Wear clothing that blends in with the surroundings.
* Take binoculars.
* Move slowly and quietly.
* Enjoy wildlife at a distance.
* Stay aware that some wildlife is dangerous.
* Don't smoke.

# MAMMALS

It is not the intent of this book to describe the many mammals that live in our forests. Listed are a few that live in our area besides deer, skunk, and racoon.

## Pronghorn Antelope

Generally found throughout the open grasslands and pinion-juniper areas here. They have exceptional eyesight and depend upon their speed, which can approach 70 mph, to escape predators. Due to their generally open habitat, antelope are easy to observe.

## Black Bears

Every bear encounter is different. In every case, bears should always be treated as potentially dangerous. More often than not, a bear will detect you first and leave the area without being seen. Bears are particularly dangerous when startled, when cubs are present, or when approached too closely. To avoid injury don't hike alone or after daylight hours. Make noises to reduce the chance of surprising a bear. Avoid all scented cosmetics, perfumes and deodorants which may attract bears. If you spot a bear, slowly back away and make a wide detour around it. If confronted by a bear, stay calm (much easier said than done). Do not run. Running may cause a bear to chase you. If a bear charges, stand your ground. Usually the bear will stop before making contact. After the bear stops, you should back away slowly, without making direct eye contact. If the bear continues, your last resort may be to play dead. Climbing trees provides little or no protection from black bears, since they're excellent climbers!

Some bears become accustomed to humans due to the offering of food. Remember the greatest attractant to bears is food. Most conflicts between people and bears are associated with the availability of food. This includes garbage, bird seed, pet foods, livestock feed, tree fruits, garden vegetables, even soap. The only kind of bear left in Arizona is the Black Bear, which despite its name can come in a variety of colors.

## Coyote

Arizona coyotes seldom weigh more than 30 pounds. Their external appearance is much like that of a shepherd dog. Coyotes are primarily carnivorous at all times of the year. Animal matter constitutes the bulk of the coyote's diet.

117

## Elk

Elk are the largest members of the deer family occurring in Arizona, sometimes exceeding 1,000 pounds. They also differ from the other deer family members by having upper canine teeth. Merriam Elk were the original breed of elk here in Arizona, but were wiped out and Elk were imported here from Yellowstone National Park in Wyoming.

## Mountain Lions (Cougar)

Few people will ever see a mountain lion in the wild as it is a very elusive mammal. Yet this beast haunts the canyons, forests, and even the desert scrub throughout virtually all of Arizona. Stalking deer, javelina, and most any other mammal it sets its mind on. Black bears have killed many times more people than mountain lions in the history of this country. An adult cougar can break the neck of a full grown elk. Cougars will run up a tree and swat a porcupine out with a single blow, then bound back down and eat the critter, spines and all, swallowing a hundred quills in a meal. Other names cougars are called are catamount or panther.

## Understanding Animal Sign

Wild animals leave various types of signs that one can keep an eye out for. Each animal is unique.

1.  Tracks indicate type of animal, their direction, and how many.
2.  Droppings (scat) can indicate whether the animal is herbivore (eats plants) or carnivore (eats meat), as well as to what type of diet they like.
3.  Territorial markings are used to indicate a domain. Scratches made in litter are made by mountain lions. Tree scratches are made by bear.
4.  Shelters - dens made by fox and badger, beds by deer and elk, nests by birds.
5.  Wallows are used by elk and javelina to roll in to keep cool and keep insects under control

A few other mammals to keep an lookout for include deer, Bobcats, javelina, squirrels, chipmunks, rabbits, racoons and skunks (*especially* the skunks!).

Avoid all wild animals. Wild animals are extremely dangerous at close range, especially during mating season or when young animals are present. Even small animals, such as chipmunks and squirrels, can be a threat if they carry rabies or other contagious diseases. And until October there's always the risk of being carried off by killer mosquitoes. So be prepared! *(Only kidding.)*

---

### How to Remove Skunk Odor from Human Skin or Pets

For pets that have been sprayed, bathe the animal in a mixture of one quart of 3% hydrogen peroxide (from a drug store), ¼ cup of baking soda (sodium bicarbonate) and a teaspoon of liquid detergent. After fifteen minutes, rinse the skin or pet with water. Repeat if necessary. The mixture must be used after mixing and *will not* work if it is stored for any length of time. **Caution:** This mixture may bleach the pet's hair.

Other options:

*Nature's Miracle Skunk Odor Remover®*, available from veterinarians or pet supply stores.
*Massengill® douche*, it's the cheapest and the easiest to find. (Stop laughing!!!)
*Vinegar and water* will also work. Vinegar is an acid which breaks down the alkaloid skunk spray.

**Note:** Avoid eye contact when using any of these methods.

---

119

# Animal Prints

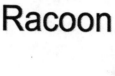

## Racoon

## Deer

## Squirrel

## Skunk

## Bear

120

# BIRDS

Many people are first exposed to birdwatching as children when their parents take them to the lakes and parks to observe ducks, swans, and geese. No puddle of water is too small to support birds.

For some it is joy enough simply to see a bird and observe its actions. Others want to comprehend its entire life-style and behavior.

Just as birds of a feather flock together, so do bird watchers. The National Audubon Society has a chapter here in Pinetop (address listed in Appendix C). Besides the Goshawks, a few of the many other engaging birds in this area include:

Northern Pintail
Ring-necked Duck
American Coot
Wild Turkey
Cooper's Hawk
Golden Eagle
Great Horned Owl
Peregrine Falcon

Ruby-crowned Kinglet
Lewis Woodpecker
Canadian Goose
Great Blue Heron
Mountain Chickadee
Mourning Dove
Osprey

Bald Eagle

# INSECTS

Chirping crickets, spectacularly patterned butterflies, and round little ladybugs need no kind words to enhance their charm. There are more than an astounding one hundred thousand kinds of insects in North American alone! Just a few of this area's insects include:

Red Admiral Butterfly
Wood Nymph Butterfly
Ladybug
Scarab Beetle
Bees *(stings)*
Wasps *(stings)*
Brown Recluse Spider *(poisonous)*
Black Widow *(poisonous)*
Tarantula *(big & ugly)*

Did you know that our word 'insect' comes from the creatures' Latin name, insectum, meaning 'notched' and refers to the indented or divided body?

**Brown Recluse Spider**

# TREES

Thoughts of tall stately trees generate visions of cool, crisp, air; clear trout streams, and lazy vacation days. Trees dominate many of our landscapes - not just in height, but also in the area they cover. The natural vegetation of more than half the continent is trees. North America has the world's *tallest* trees, the most *massive* trees, and the *oldest* trees.

Our area boasts the largest continuous stand of Ponderosa Pine trees in the United States. Some of this area's most common trees include:

The Ponderosa pine also called Western Yellow pine, Blackjack, or Yellow Belly, has needles 5 to 10 inches long. Attached to twig in bundles of three. Bark is rough and dark on young trees; orangeish and smoother on older trees. Specimens may exceed 150 feet in height and be four feet plus through at the base.

Arizona pine is also called the Apache pine. Its needles are from 9 to 15 inches in length, with three or four in a bundle. Found above 5000 feet in elevation and isn't common.

White Fir is a large evergreen tree with short, flat, single needles which usually grow horizontally from opposite sides of the twig. The conical shape of the tree and the bluish cast of needles cause frequent confusion with the Blue Spruce which is seen at lower elevations. Its cone is smooth without bracts or spines.

Douglas Fir is an evergreen tree with needles generally smaller than the White Fir which grow all around the twig. The cone has three-lobed, papery protruding bracts.

Quaking Aspen has tall straight trunk with smooth white bark, small leafs, and a rounded base. It is not too common below 7000 feet and is a beaver's favorite food.

Do you know how pines reproduce? Pines, like other conifers, usually have two kinds of cones. In spring, the wind carries pollen from the short-lived male structures (often on the lower branches) to the female cones. The female cones become brown and woody as seeds ripen on the scales. The cones open and release their seeds at maturity, usually in autumn of the second year.

Gambel Oak's leaves are lobed, rounded, turn brown, and drop in Autumn. These trees generally don't grow more than 30 feet tall and their bark is rough and gray. Their fruit is the acorn.

Arizona White Oak, sometimes called Arizona Life Oak, is an evergreen. Its leaves may take several forms on the same tree; usually holly-like or oval with rough margins. Its fruit is the acorn.

(Again, space doesn't permit the listing of the many more shrubs, grasses, and annuals that make up this area's forests. In addition, one may find an abundance of lichen, mosses, ferns, and parasites.)

The Douglas in the name of "Douglas Fir" refers to David Douglas, a 19th century botanical explorer.

# POISON OAK

There are many, many plants in the wild that are more or less poisonous if eaten. Know exactly what you are doing before you eat any part of any wild plant, including, most especially, any mushroom. The only general first aid rule for plant poisoning is to drink water and induce vomiting.

Much more common is another kind of poisoning: the brief, inconsequential sting of nettle or the unbearable itch of poison oak and similar toxic plants. Poison oak or ivy are hardly a danger to your life, but it can certainly take the pleasure out of your day. Poison ivy has been spotted along Billy Creek. The best field mark to look for when looking for poison oak is its leaves. The saying *"If it has three, leave it be"* is true. Leaves are grouped in threes. Each group of three leaflets grows out at a different point along the stem; the clusters are "alternate," not "opposite."

Over a million people each year come down with cases of poison oak. Only about half the population is allergic -- maybe you're in the lucky half. Your best defense is soap and water. The irritant saps are water-soluble, so you can often head off an eruption by washing just after exposure. Once the reaction has begun, you can

Poison Ivy

suppress the itching somewhat with poison oak lotions.

The saps of the poison oaks are transported by anything they touch, including boots, clothes, packs, and car seats. They stay potent for quite some time. To avoid infecting others or yourself for a second time, wash suspect items thoroughly with soap and water.

# WILD FLOWERS

You'll need a good book, one complete with photos and detailed descriptions, to take with you when you go wild flower gathering. The following are some and by no means all of the wild flowers you may see.

Aralias
Asters
Cattails
Fleabanes
Groundsels
Indian Paintbrush
Irises
Lupine
Manzanitas
Mistletoe
Phlox
Primroses
Ragweeds

Snow Plants
Starflowers
Thistles
Wood Sorrels
Skunk Bush
Gooseberry Currant
Wild Parsley
Pussy Toes
Golden Pea
Wild Grape
Bluebells
Wild Raspberries
Indian Pipe

# MUSHROOMS

Whether or not you are already enthusiastic about these lowly plants, once you start to notice their beauty and diversity you will surely find them intriguing. Exploring for mushrooms, identifying them, and learning about how they live and grow give a great deal of pleasure to many people, but others are attracted to mushrooms because they are free and exotic items of food.

And, just like the warning about poison oak and ivy, I think it prudent to include this warning about mushrooms. Eating wild mushrooms is extremely risky. Fatally poisonous species as well as ones that will make you unpleasantly ill grow throughout North America, and no general rule allows discrimination between those that are edible and those that are inedible or worse. No wild mushroom should be eaten in any amount or in any form unless identified by an expert and declared safe.

Mushroom hunting is an activity for all seasons, and there are even a few species, such as the Winter Mushroom, that "sprout" only when the weather is cold. But Fall, especially after rain, is a prime time for finding mushrooms; wet Springs are second best. Mushrooms form part of the enormous group of organisms we call fungi - organisms defined by their habits of growth and their inability to make their own food.

The following mushrooms are ones I found in August of 1999 (an exceptional monsoon summer) while hiking the Lake Mountain spur trail Four Springs. I collected a sample of each, took them home, checked out a book from the library and proceeded to match them with the photos in the book:

Casear's

Grisette

Chanterelle

Honey

Cone-shaped Hygrophorus

King Bolete

Crowned Clavaria

Lobster

False Truffle

Orange Hypomyces

Greenish-Yellow Tricholoma

Waxy Laccaria

There are over 30 more listed in the book that are supposed to be in this area as well. To enjoy searching for them yourself, I recommend the Reader's Digest North American Wildlife. A reminder, that it isn't the intent of this book to include pictures of every animal, tree, plant, etc it mentions.

# HEALTH & TRAIL CARE

## Lightning Awareness

Thunderstorms bring beauty, excitement and much needed water, but they also bring risk. Thunderstorms are accompanied by dangerous (and sometimes deadly) lightening. Summer storms (July - September) in the White Mountains occur frequently.

Lightening is a powerful electrical charge from a thunderstorm that can kill instantly. If your hair stands on end or your skin prickles, an electrical charge is building near you and lightening may strike you.

While on hikes, watch for locations that may offer some protection. Listen for thunder, watch for lightening and observe the direction of the storm movement. If thunder is near you, recognize the danger and take cover.

* Stay away from rims, rocky outcrops, other open areas, metal guard rails, lone trees, tall trees, poles, bicycles and bodies of water.
* Get in a building or car quickly.
* Don't touch or be in contact with any metal in the vehicle or structure.

If storms are near and shelter is unavailable, be calm and use good judgment. Lightening safety is sometimes a matter of taking the less risky alternative.

In a forest seek a group of small trees surrounded by tall trees or look for a dry lower ground (ravine, depression, etc.) Avoid individual tall trees.

In open space, become a smaller target. Seek lower ground and assume the 'lightning safety position.' Crouch on the balls of your feet with heels together, head down, hands covering ears. Hands shouldn't touch the ground. Don't lie flat on the ground. Spread out of other people, if possible.

## Clothing

Clothing is a matter of common sense and comfort. The clothes on your back and in your day pack are a large part of your comfort and safety. They are daytime protection from cold and from wind; from soaking chilling rain and even snow; from heat and burning ultraviolet rays; from 'no-see-ems bugs', mosquitoes, poison oak or ivy, and thick, scratching underbrush. An essential item not taken can mean discomfort or even danger.

There is no such thing as a standard list of clothing. People vary. Every hiker works out the combinations that are right for him or her. And the wilderness itself - from hot to cold, from wet to dry, from calm to battering wind - varies most of all.

A good combination would include a T-shirt, a long-sleeved shirt, a down vest or wind-breaker, and a rain parka. A hat is also handy to keep the high altitude sun off your head and out of your eyes. Any type of pants will do. Cotton/synthetic and plain cotton fabrics are cooler and more comfortable than others. Denims are popular and cheap. Pants should be loose fitting and in good condition. Avoid wide cuffed or bell-bottoms. Shorts are nice, but watch out for sunburn. Irritant plants and insects, as well as underbrush, can make wearing shorts a regret.

Personally, I tend to favor pieces of clothing that do a single job to those that try to serve several purposes at once. If you have both a light insulated jacket and a shell, you can wear the jacket alone when it's cool and still; the shell alone when it is not so cold but blowing; both together when you need the greatest protection. But if you brought a monstrous down-stuffed parka that is shell and jacket in one, you have no choice. You either wear the entire thing or you don't.

In our area we are blessed with a temperate four season climate. Summers are kept cool with a monsoon season (rain) usually in July and August. These rains come quickly and hit randomly. It is not unusual to be enjoying a picnic in sunny 80 degree weather and 10 miles down the road there is a downpour.

Remember to start with your basic outfit and then, ask yourself: What else, if anything, do I need to add for *cold*? What shell or shells should I add for *wind* and *wet*?

## Foot Care

Pay attention to your feet. The more miles you walk, the more serious you have to be about their care. One of the most important things you can do to care for your skin is to give it air. If you are walking an hour or more, stop each hour, take off the shoes and socks and air out your feet.

Wear good 'walking (not running) shoes', absorbent socks and practice foot maintenance. Toenails should always be trimmed. The more you walk, the more the foot stretches, and long nails can cause toe and nail problems.

The key to exercising is to never go beyond the point where within 24 hours, you cannot go out and do the same workout again. If you are so sore or have hurt yourself so that you can't repeat the workout then you've done too much.

## Trail Dos and Don'ts

Be kind to the environment. Your presence, and that of others, has an impact on many environmental elements. To prevent potential damage to the environment you are asked to:
* Respect the land. Stay on designated paths.
* Avoid wet or muddy trails.
* Don't cut switchbacks, take shortcuts, or create new trails.
* Keep your party small to avoid impacting the area.
* Take only pictures, leave only footprints. Don't take living souvenirs.
* Don't leave any trash behind (includes used toilet paper). To assist in trail maintenance, carry a trash bag and pick up any litter.
* Keep dogs on leash and pick up their droppings for proper disposal elsewhere.
* Bring plenty of water, especially during the summer months.
* Don't tease any animal. Wildlife should be admired and treated with respect.
* Don't bury trash!  Animals dig it up. (Cigarette butts, pull-tabs, and gum wrappers are litter too!)
* Try to pack out trash left by others. Set a good example!

## No Trace Ethic

Because most of us do not live in the out-of-doors all the time, we unknowingly do things that do *not* reflect a "No Trace" ethic.
*      Bright colored outdoor gear dotting the landscape.
*      Large groups traveling and camping together.

* Traveling off trail, causing scars, trampled vegetation and soil erosion; especially in meadows and near lakes and streams.
* Campfire scars.
* Human waste and garbage scattered about.
* Loud noise which disturbs wildlife and other visitors.

To avoid over-regulation, wilderness management must rely on the wilderness user (you and I) to assume the responsibility to practice appropriate back country techniques. It requires the ultimate in the assumption of responsibility for one's own safety and well-being as well as for the well-being of the land itself.

## A Word to Backpackers

Should you want to prolong a hike over the period of a day I've included a suggested list of 'What To Take' in the chapter titled Reference Lists (page 21). With many trails interconnecting, it is very possible to enjoy a few days of backpacking on the connecting trails mentioned in this book.

Low-impact camping was once merely a courtesy, but it is on the verge of becoming a requirement, both to protect the landscape and to preserve a sense of solitude for others. The most important rules:

* Camp out of sight of lakes and trails.
* Do not build a campfire. Cook on a backpacking stove.
* Wash 100 feet from any lake or stream.
* Camp on rock or sand, never on meadow vegetation.
* Pack out garbage - don't burn or bury it.

## Trail Courtesy

Mountain bikes should yield to all users, hikers should yield to horses, and horses always have the right-of-way. Courtesy toward others helps everyone enjoy their outdoor experience. Excessive noise, unleashed pets, and damaged natural surroundings create a negative atmosphere. While traveling on trails keep the noise level down. Radio and tape players do not belong. Uphill hikers have the right-of-way.

Keep pets under control at all times. No one wants to have someone's pet running through the area frightening people and wildlife.

## Additional Maps

White Mountains Trails System Guide, USGS topographic maps and the Apache-Sitgreaves National Forest map may aide in your hiking. The trails do not appear on the topo or national forest maps. Trails frequently follow old logging roads and may cross roads open to motorized traffic. If you become lost, backtrack to a known landmark. Read the following section titled "What to Do If You Are Lost Or Injured" on page 7. Aforementioned maps are customarily available at Chambers of Commerce, Parks & Rec. Depts., and Forest Service Stations.

## Group Size

Small groups of less than 10 people are ideal. Smaller groups are more desirable in open areas. When traveling, no matter by what means, make an effort to stay on the trails. Switchbacks are the most abused portion of the trail system. A switchback is a reversal in trail direction. Many people cut switchbacks trying to save time and energy. They are only creating a new scar on the hillside which will cause soil erosion and many problems for work crews later. Avoid traveling through meadows and wet areas. These fragile places will show the impact of foot prints and group travel much longer than forested or rocky areas.

## Trash

Practice tearing packages open only part way. You will have only one piece of trash, not two. Make an effort to pocket all of your trash, including cigarette butts & used toilet paper for emptying later. NEVER bury your trash, animals have a tendency to dig it up. If you packed it in full you can certainly pack it out empty. Try to pack out trash left by others. Set a good example!

## The Land Beyond the Trailhead

How much of our remaining wild country, its woods, its trails, its animals, its waters, will we deliberately keep the way it is? How much will we make ours forever? How much will we let go?

Wilderness and trail systems belong to everyone. Its value is not only for those who make direct and obvious use of it. Entry to the world of trails is not hard. There are few Americans who are physically prevented from making the effort. There are many - indeed, the large majority - who have so far not tried. Some just aren't attracted and others are content to have their wilderness secondhand in books, photographs, or via television, or the Internet. But still others stay home simply because they don't know how to start or they have an exaggerated idea of the difficulties, the discomforts, the expense.

Hiking is probably not for everyone, but it may be for a good number of people who have not yet found it out. There seems to be in many people a kind of hunger for wilderness, which once aroused, is never to be satisfied by any substitute. It is akin to the same spiritual emptiness we feel which can only be filled by God.

The American Hiking Society estimates that 66 million hikers use the nation's trails, taking at least 5 million trips a year. The demand is on the increase.

One of the chief pleasures of the land beyond the trailhead has always been the independence of the traveler and the freedom from formal rules. One thing is unmistakable. Restriction will come soonest, and in the most annoying form, in the places where the hikers themselves have failed. The job of protecting wilderness and wildlife belongs largely to us who enjoy it. Each of us has the power to keep problems from occurring. We can each make a contribution to help. The demand for wilderness is great and growing - so much greater, then, the need to protect our only, irreplaceable supply. Each of us can lend some small individual weight to the cause of protecting what is unprotected now.

> **One more thing!**
> Before you set out, pause to sign in at the trailhead register; if one is provided. Even though you may have left word with someone, the register is still the final record of who you are and where you are going.

It is one thing to think about the dwindling of the American wilderness. It is quite another to watch it dwindle, to see the same piece of land be sold and a city overrunning it.

People react to this experience in many ways. Some are angered. Some are grieved. Some are resigned. Some make it a project to see as many beautiful places as they can "before they're all spoiled." But these people have in common - too many of them - the belief that these changes are inevitable and that nothing anyone can do will stop them. If you can't even (as the old saying goes) fight City Hall - then what hope can there be in taking on a large and determined government agency?

It also happens to be dead wrong! If there's anything we should have learned from the history of American conservation, it is that, if you have to, you can fight, or at any rate, influence the proverbial City Hall! "Inevitable" processes can in fact be changed or turned aside. And the force that does it is usually nothing more than the letter of opinion written by the citizen to somebody who has the power to decide.

So if you have a strong opinion about what's happening to our wilderness, don't sit on it. Write! Write to the managing agency, your representative in Congress or an environmental organization that shares the same concerns you do.

If only the small proportion of today's hikers did speak up, their common voice would be very loud indeed! There is more than a little satisfaction in doing something, however slight, to protect the future of a place you have enjoyed.

Orange Hypomyces
Grisette
Earth Star

# HIDE & SEEK

CAN YOU FIND THESE OBJECTS?
Keep your eyes open and see if you can find these. Space is provided for you to make notes.

# AREA INFORMATION

Transition Zone
Mogollon Rim
Our National Forests
Apache-Sitgreaves Forest
AZ Fish & Game
Navajo County
White Mountain Apache Reservation
City of Pinetop-Lakeside
City of Show Low
Rodeo-Chediski Fire
Reporting Violations

## Transition Zone

C. Hart Merriam, was a naturalist who traveled through Arizona with the early explorers and the military in the mid-late 1800s. He found that vegetation changed along with elevation, temperature, and amount of precipitation. Mountains are determined by elevation and topography and vegetation. He is credited with coming up with the Life Zone Class of Arizona's vegetation. Our area falls into the Transition Zone. The following are the Life Zone Classes:

| | |
|---|---|
| Arctic-Alpine Zone | 11500 - 14000' + |
| Hudsonian | 9500' - 11500' |
| Canadian | 8000' - 9500' |
| *Transition | 6000 - 8000' |
| Upper Sonora | 4000' - 6000' |
| Lower Sonora | 1000' - 4000' |

*Our area has upper Sonoran's pinion, juniper, Transition area's ponderosa pine, and the Canadian's fir and spruce vegetation. Cacti from the Sonora elevation can even be found.

## Mogollon Rim

Its been said that to visit the Mogollon Rim is to stand on the edge of the world. For more than 200 miles, the Mogollon Rim cuts across north-central Arizona; a bold, rugged, dramatic, limestone escarpment that rises thousands of feet above the desert shrub of the Tonto Basin. It is easily the most dominant geologic feature in central Arizona. It marks the end, in a dramatic fashion, of the Colorado Plateau, and the beginning of one of the basin and range provinces of the Arizona desert.

The Mogollon Rim is deeply rooted in the consciousness of travelers. Captain John G. Bourke, who traveled along the crest of the Rim in 1871 called it, "a strange freak of nature, a mountain canted up on one side." It is an area whose roots are of prehistoric peoples, Apaches and Yavapais, miners and prospectors, soldiers, cattlemen and sheep men, outlaws, and bloody feuds. Its rich history is surpassed only by its magnificent scenery.

The Rim country is also a haven for those who love the outdoors. It is comprised of portions of three national forests: the Apache-Sitgreaves, the Coconino, and the Tonto. This country is a beautiful but fragile land. Enjoy it, but treat it with the respect it deserves. Future generations enjoyment depend upon you.

## Our National Forests

*"We administer 230,000 acres of land and have dumping occur throughout most of it . . They dump in it like it's going to go away - only it doesn't ever go away."*

~Walter Scott, U. S. Forest Service
Reprinted from Friday, July 30, 1999
NavApache Independent Newspaper, page 7B

The Forest Service maintains the habitats for wildlife in the forests under its jurisdiction, but has very little to do with the regulation of hunting and fishing, since this is the province of the Arizona Game and Fish Department. The two agencies cooperate in attempting to maintain a balance between the production and harvesting of the many game animals inhabiting the forests.

Each year the national forests in our state are visited by several million people seeking escape from the heat and hustle of the big cities at lower elevations. The Forest Service has built and maintains many picnic and camp grounds throughout the region.

Of all the problems faced by the Forest Service, man is by far the greatest problem. Thoughtless littering, vandalism and carelessness with fire result in the expenditure of much money and many man-hours by our forest rangers that easily could be put to much better use.

The Forest Service subscribes to the philosophy of multiple use and sustained yield in its management of your national forests. Conservation here means making the wisest use of the natural resources of the forests without permanently impairing their ability to keep producing. Our beautiful national forests are the source of:

* Three-fourths of the water for the western portion of the United States.
* Home to 60 percent of the birds and animals that live in the U.S.A.
* Supply ½ of the soft-wood needed for homes and paper for schools and businesses.
* Supply 40% of all outdoor recreation and 84% of all wilderness areas.

## Apache-Sitgreaves Forest History

The Apache and Sitgreaves National Forest is one of 11 National Forests in the Southwestern Region of Arizona and New Mexico. The Forest encompasses two million acres of magnificent mountain country located along the Mogollon Rim and in the White Mountains of east-central Arizona.

The Sitgreaves National forest was named for Captain Lorenzo Sitgreaves, a government topographical engineer who conducted the first scientific expedition across Arizona in the early 1850s. The Apache National Forest is named for the Apache Indian tribes still residing on the neighboring reservations.

There are over 200,000 acres of wilderness and primitive areas within the Forest. Travel within these areas is restricted to foot or horseback. The Forest provides habitat (food and shelter) for 411 species of wildlife. Species include most big game animals and a wide variety of birds, waterfowl, and fish. Thanks to the Wilderness Act of 1964, some of the most striking country in the United States has been preserved.

The Wilderness Act states: *"It is hereby declared to be the policy of Congress to secure for the American people . . . the benefits of an enduring resource of wilderness. . . where the earth and its community of life are untrammeled by man, where man himself is a visitor who does not remain."*

## AZ Fish & Game

Wildlife management programs benefit all who enjoy wildlife, yet receive no general state tax money. Hunting and fishing licenses, special fees, designated federal funds and a checkoff on state tax forms (for non-game management) pay for most of the department's activities.

Over $650 million is spent every year on wildlife-related recreation in this state. This amount doesn't include monies spent by tourists, hikers, and campers whose recreational experience is enhanced by wildlife.

## Navajo County

Navajo county covers over six million acres and is the fourth largest county in the state. The county border's extend north through the Navajo and Hopi reservations to the Utah state line, south to the White Mountains, the Apache Reservation and along the Mongollon Rim. In the north, semi-arid, high plateau grassland reveal rugged desert beauty. In contrast, the southern end is heavily wooded with Juniper, Pinion, and Ponderosa Pine. The Indian reservations in Navajo county include the world renowned scenic Monument Valley, historical Fort Apache, and the ancient Hopi villages.

## White Mountain Apache Reservation

Our neighbor adjacent to Pinetop is the White Mountain Apache Reservation covering 1,664,874 acres of some of the most beautiful, pristine, and fertile forest land ever seen. The Indians were the first travelers and residents of the mountain. Recent evidence points to their migration into the area about 900-1000 years ago. It was not until the 1800's that the Mormon pioneers with their wagon trains settled this beautiful land. Prior to that time we can only trace back to trappers and explorers that may have come this way.

Coronado, searching for gold trooped through the White Mountains in 1540. Spanish colonists in Nuevo Mexico came to know the Indians well. They called them Apaches de Navahu, from a Zuni word which meant "enemy."

To protect trade routes and encourage settlement, the U.S. Army, in 1870, established an outpost at Camp Mogollon (later called Camp Apache, then Fort Apache).

In 1870, Cordon E. Cooley was hired at the fort as an Army Scout. Because of Cooley, this region was spared the bloodshed of Indian Wars which took place elsewhere. He married the chief's two daughters, Molly and Cora of the White Mountain Apache Chief Pedro. In 1878, after completing his Army service he and partner, Henry Huning, settled along Show Low Creek and built a house, installed a sawmill and started ranching.

In the same year, William L. Penrod and his wife, were called by the Church of Jesus Christ of Latter-Day Saints to help colonize the Arizona Territory. They arrived in Show Low on Christmas Eve, 1878, with their nine children. Penrod found work on the Cooley Ranch. It wasn't long before logging became a vital part of the development of this part of the country. In 1886, the Penrod family relocated to the Pinetop area and established a small shingle mill business.

## The City of Pinetop-Lakeside

Pinetop-Lakeside has received American Hiking Society's Trail Town U.S.A. Award" and the TRACKS volunteer organization has received state awards for their outstanding efforts to build and improve the White Mountain Trail System.

Pinetop-Lakeside boasts a growing year round population of 8,000, swelling up to 25,000 - 30,000 in the summer. Pinetop-Lakeside rests at 7200' elevation. The White Mountain Indian Reservation borders on the south.

When the Penrod family relocated to Pinetop in 1886, they sold their farming produce to the personnel at Fort Apache, thus causing Pinetop to grow into a town with a post office, store, and a small school.

Lakeside is actually an older community than Pinetop. Hans Hansen Senior was called in 1884 to be bishop of a ward (Mormons) that extended from Linden to Fort Apache and settled in Lakeside in the Woodland Park district. He and his son Hans Jr. were masons. They did rock work at Fort Apache and Whiteriver. All the two-story brick homes in this area can be traced to them.

The first store in Lakeside was run by Billy Scorse, an Englishman, for whom Billy Creek was named. One spring day in 1906, six men sat in the sun at the south end of Niels Hansen's barn and named the town "Lakeside." They were John Fish, who bought out Billy Scorse, John Hansen, Joseph Peterson, Louis Johnson, and Alof Larson.

After the First World War, the tourist and summer resident businesses blossomed, and as time went on, Pinetop-Lakeside became a well known resort area with cabins, motels, and top restaurants. The historic step of incorporation was taken by Pinetop-Lakeside in 1984.

## The City of Show Low ~ Named By The Turn Of A Card

Show Low is considered the commercial and tourism center of the White Mountains. It sits aside the Mogollon Rim. The town was established in 1870 and incorporated in 1953. Located in southern Navajo County at an elevation of 6,330 feet, the city is 175 miles northwest of Phoenix and 195 miles north of Tucson.

Show Low received its name when partners C. E. Cooley, a famous Indian scout and Marion Clark settled their land in 1870, fencing off some 100,000 acres with barbed wire. The present townsite was part of this large ranch. Several years later, the two partners had a disagreement and decided there was not enough room for both of them in their settlement. The two men agreed to dissolve their partnership with a game of poker called "Seven Up" to decide who was to move. According to the story, they played all night. Clark said, *"If you can show low, you win."* Cooley cut the deck, and came up with the deuce of clubs and replied, *"Show low it is."* Hence the name of the town and its main street.

# RODEO-CHEDISKI FIRE

**June 18 - July 6, 2002** - The day the Rodeo Fire started, the Bureau of Indian Affairs (BIA) fire officials rejected offers of help. Four days later 30,000 people were evacuated from Show Low, Pinetop Lakeside, McNary, Linden, Pinedale, Clay Springs, Airipine and Heber/Overgaard. The first fire began near the rodeo grounds just northeast of Cibecue on the Ft. Apache Reservation. An out of work firefighter by the name of Leonard Gregg, 29, of Cibecue started it to earn income fighting it. The BIA firefighters believed they could hold the fire, but bone-dry fuels, extreme drought and gusty winds enabled it to outrace all efforts. By nightfall, the fire had burned an estimate 100 - 300 acres and the BIA firefighters stopped believing they could contain it.

More than 15 miles away, the Chediski Fire was set early Thursday morning, June 20, by Valinda Jo Elliot, a lost motorist, trying to flag down a news helicopter. Left unattended it rapidly consumed 2,000 acres. On Sunday, June 23, the two fires combined into one monster. On Tuesday, June 25, President Bush arrived to view the monster and to sign a federal disaster declaration.

The Rodeo-Chediski Fire crept as close as one quarter of a mile from the Show Low city limits. It burned 468,638 acres. The number of structures burned were 426. A total of 4,447 personnel were assigned to the fire and worked at putting it out at a cost of $43 million. It will cost that much to repair environmental damage. Untold millions were lost in timber and tourism business. President Bush pledged $20 million to help defray the costs. The fire was fully contained on July 6. No one was killed or seriously injured. The Rodeo-Chediski Fire was the largest fire in the State of Arizona's history.

# REPORTING VIOLATIONS

*"I have become all things to all men so that by all possible means I might save some" (1 Corinthians 9:22).*

The White Mountains Trail System (W.M.T.S.) is designed for non-motorized travel: hiking, mountain bike, and equestrian use. Please report violations of people using motorized vehicles (i.e., four wheelers, motorcycles).

Report Violations at the following offices:

AZ Game & Fish Dept., Pinetop 367-4281
Lakeside Ranger District      368-5111
Show Low Police Dept.        537-4365

If you see violations take a moment and jot down the following:

```
Date: _____ Time: _____
Vehicle: _____
License #: _____ Color: _____
Make: _____ Model: _____
Violation Observed:     _____
_____
```

## To report illegal dumping, please call 1-800) NOT-DUMP.

# APPENDICES

A.  How to Become a Child of God

B.  Trails Listed in Order of Their Trail Number

C.  Addresses and Phone Numbers

D.  Suggested Reference Guides

E.  List of Maps, Photos & Drawings

F.  Scripture List

# APPENDIX A

## HOW TO BECOME A CHILD OF GOD

It is my prayer that God has used this book to bless and encourage you. You may sense God's Spirit tugging at your heart while you are hiking and wonder how you can have a personal relationship with the Lord Jesus Christ. The Bible clearly explains how you can become a child of God and receive eternal life.

God loves us as a Father loves a child. His desire is that each one of us have a personal relationship with Him. His plan for us is quite simple.

> *"For God so loved the world, that He gave His only begotten Son, that whoever believes in Him should not perish, but have eternal life"* (John 3:16).

Our sinful nature separates us from being able to have a relationship with a holy God.

> *"All have sinned and fall short of the glory of God"* (Romans 3:23).
> *"The wages of sin is death"* (Spiritual death and separation from God) *(Romans 6:23).*

Jesus Christ died on the cross in our place to bear the penalty of our sin. His death and resurrection bridge the gap between God and man. This enables us to enter into a loving relationship with God.

> *"God demonstrates His own love toward us, in that while we were yet sinners, Christ died for us"* (Romans 5:8).
> *"Jesus said to him, "I am the way, the truth and the life, no one comes to the Father except through Me"* (John 14:6).

We must *each* individually make a decision to believe these facts *by faith.*

> *"By grace you have been saved through faith; and that not of yourselves, it is the gift of God; not as a result of works that no one should boast"* (Ephesians 2:8,9).

No matter who you are, at this very moment you can accept Jesus Christ as your Lord and Savior. Quietly pray this prayer from a sincere heart:

"Lord Jesus, thank you for dying on the cross for my sins. I open my heart to you and ask you to be my Savior and Lord. Thank you for forgiving my sins and granting me eternal life. I give you control of my life and ask you to make me the person you created me to be. Thank you dear Lord! Amen!"

*"Yet to all who received Him, to those who believed in His name, He gave the right to become children of God" (John 1:12).*

# APPENDIX B

## Trails Listed in Order of Their Trail Number
*Trails without assigned numbers are not listed.*

| | |
|---|---|
| 107 | Blue Ridge |
| 130 | General Crook |
| 608 | Ice Cave |
| 610 | Big Springs |
| 615 | Rim View |
| 617 | Pintail Lake Wetlands |
| 629 | Land of the Pioneers |
| 629a | Four Springs |
| 631 | Los Burros |
| 631a | Chipmunk Springs |
| 632 | Country Club |
| 632a | Iron Horse |
| 633 | Springs |
| 635 | Panorama |
| 636 | Timber Mesa |
| 636a | The Sawmill |
| 636b | The Flume |
| 637 | Buena Vista |
| 638 | Los Caballos |
| 638a | The Chihuahua Pine |
| 640 | Juniper Ridge |
| 640a | The Lookout |
| 641 | Ghost of the Coyotes |

# APPENDIX C
## ADDRESSES & PHONE NUMBERS

**Emergency 911**
*All area codes (928) unless otherwise indicated.*

**American Hiking Society**
1701 18th St., NW
Washington D.C. 20009

**White Mountain Audubon Society**
P. O. Box 3043
Pinetop, AZ 85935

**Apache Wildlife & Outdoor Recreation**
338-4385

**Lakeside Ranger District**
RR 3, Box B-50
Pinetop-Lakeside, AZ 85929
368-5111

**USDA Forest Service**
Arizona & New Mexico
517 Gold Ave., SW
Albuquerque, NM 87102
505) 842-3292 / 3236

**Apache-Sitgreaves National Forests**
P. O. Box 640
Springerville, AZ 85938
333-4301

**Arizona Trail Association**
602) 252-4794

**Leave No Trace, Inc.**
P. O. Box 997
Boulder, CO 80306
800) 332-4100

**TRACKS**
Pinetop-Lakeside Chamber of Commerce
368-6700

**Pinetop-Lakeside Parks & Recreation**
1360 N. Niels Hansen Lane
Lakeside, AZ 85929
368-6700

**Fool Hollow Lake Recreation Area**
P. O. Box 2588
Show Low, AZ 85901
537-3680

**Road & Weather Information**
537-ROAD

**Show Low Chamber of Commerce**
81 E. Deuce of Clubs
Show Low, AZ
537-2326

# APPENDIX D

## Suggested Reference Guides

The Bible - King James & New International Version

White Mountain Trail System Guide Book, Lakeside Forest Station

The Mogollon Rim, Rim Guide Hiking Map, Arizona Highways

Apache-Sitgreaves National Forest Pocket Guide

Arizona Wildlife View, Heritage Issue, October 1992

Hiking Central Arizona, Don R. Kiefer

North American Wildlife, The Reader's Digest Association

Flowers of the Southwest Mountains, Leslie P. Arnberger

A Field Guide to the Mammals, Williams Burt & Richard
  Grossenheider

Animal Tracks of the Southwest, Chris Stall, The Mountaineers

Complete Field Guide to American Wildlife, Henry Hill Collins Jr.,
  Harper and Row

Birds of the Apache-Sitgreaves National Forest: A Checklist, White
  Mountain Audubon Society

Rim Guide Hiking Map, Arizona Highways

# APPENDIX E
## List of Maps, Photos & Drawings
*Trail maps are not listed.*

# APPENDIX F
## Scripture Reference List

Acts 17:25
1 Thessalonians 5:18
1 Samuel 16:7
1 Corinthians 9:22
1 Peter 2:24
1 John 1:9
1 Chronicles 23:30
2 Corinthians 10:3
Deuteronomy 5:33
Ephesians 4:25
Genesis 1:1
Hebrews 10:19, 11:3, 12:11
Isaiah 40:3,4
Jeremiah 17:10
John 4:3b, 3:16, 4:24
Luke 11:4
Matthew 6:22, 3:10, 5:3, 4:4, 3:3b
Numbers 22:24
Proverbs 16:3, 1:7, 16:5
Psalm 9:10, 69:30, 17:5, 48:9, 104:5, 96:6, 1:1, 107:1, 63:8, 8:3,4, 46:10, 119:101, 19:1; 24:1
Revelation 19:1b
Romans 10:13, 1:20

# INDEX

City and trail names appear in boldface.
*See Appendix E for listing of maps, photos, and illustrations.*

# ABOUT THE AUTHOR
# LAURIE DEE ACREE

*"The earth is the LORD's, and the fullness thereof; the world,*
*and they that dwell therein"* (Psalm 24:1).

It is so relaxing to take a hike. I consider myself blessed to live in the beautiful White Mountains where there are more than a thousand miles of trails within the national forest and city limits and not a telephone pole in sight nor the cacophony of airplanes overhead.

I seriously began hiking in 1980. I married a hiker that year and we went backpacking in Yosemite for our honeymoon. I've hiked in six western European countries, Mexico, throughout the New England states, the Rockies, the Cascades, the Sierra Nevadas, the Lagunas, National Parks – and the White Mountains. When I am not hiking, I am drawing or painting. As an artist, I strive to capture wildlife on paper or canvas and have included several of my drawings in this book.

Author & husband,
Sept. 2001, Yellowstone National Park

**ORDERS**: Should you need to order
more copies please contact the author.
Home Phone # 928) 537-7706
600 W. Reidhead Street
Show Low AZ 85901

ISBN 141201111-6

9 781412 011112